'Signs and Circumstances'
A Study of Allegory in Chaucer's Canterbury Tales.

Alan Hughes

British Library Cataloguing-in-publication data. A catalogue record for this book is available from the British Library.

Copyright ©2004 by Alan Hughes.
Revised Edition 2020.

First published by AlaNia, Tan y Gaer, Pentrefoelas,
Conwy.
LL24 0LE.
email: oahughes3@btinternet.com
ISBN 0 9544491 0 X

Printed and bound by CPI Group (UK) Ltd, Croyden. CR0 4YY

Alan Hughes has asserted his right under the Copyright, Design and Patents Act 1988 to be identified as the author of this work.

Acknowledgements

This book would not have been completed without the backing of my wife. Especially important was her ensuring that a quiet corner of our busy home was kept undisturbed during that time when I undertook the unravelling of what initially appeared to be Chaucer's complex allegorical patterns. Though very late in the day, to our six children I ask your forgiveness for not having been as attentive a father as I probably should have been in your early years. It would be pleasing if my parents remained alive, for they were a great source of inspirational strength in the dark periods of my critical bewilderment, those days of my feelings of incompetence and the accompanying impatience.

To Coleg Harlech, the remarkably 'Second Chance' college for those such as myself that had missed out on their early education, I will forever be grateful for their initiating what has become my increasing love of good literature. The support of Gladstone's Library at Hawarden also needs to be acknowledged, for without the generosity of their scholarship that provided me with an ideal location for study, and along with this an access to their vast collection of books, the details required to gain my Masters Degree in the subject of medieval allegory would not have been so readily gathered.

Introduction

The reader will find here a description of the investigative method I intend to pursue in this book, and with it comes the reasons for my having chosen such an unusual allegorical reading of the *Canterbury Tales*. Rather than the present considerations of the *CT* being a mainly humourous criticism of humanity's corrupted ideals, I will attempt to keep the theory I put forward within a close relationship to the spirit of those figured depictions that, in my understanding of the subject matter, progresses us steadily towards the directly expressed and resounding conclusions to be found in the Parson's summarising tale. Those religious values that underline Chaucer's belief of God being the establisher of all the worldly bounty that forms our reality; and with this a vision of the Christian pathway towards discovery of the kinder nature of historical development by means of discerning what should constantly be the charitable motivations in our personal and social actions.

Throughout this attempt to determine how the *Canterbury Tales* is best understood, I have increasingly grown in conviction that reading the work within a framework of an historical allegory presents the best means of clarifying what can otherwise be the work's more perplexing passages. Initially I need to firmly repeat that O. B.

Hardison's study into such half-hidden matter (sentences) as form the matter of medieval writings informs us that Boccaccio's work of poetical criticism contains the following heading: 'It Is a Fool's Notion That Poets Convey No Meaning Beneath the Surface of Their Fictions.'[1]

Academic opposition to an allegorical reading as I will be suggesting here forms the consensus approach of present-day critical readers into the *Canterbury Tales*. What I propose will therefore need to convincingly satisfy that a hidden level of historical meanings exists within the *CT*, and that the understanding of this oblique form of presentation is of paramount importance if we are to gain a fuller enjoyment of the work. That is I believe a figurative study best explains those passages presently taken to be dark or at best ambiguous when solely given surface explanations. Very obviously the acceptability of this investigation depends on how credible and consistently the linkages that I present progresses us through the hidden levels being claimed. If to be successful in my unfolding of the text it will need to provide increasing evidence that another, and a more significant allegorical dimension, underlies the surface details of the historical background I am

---

[1] Hardison, O.B., *Medieval Literary Criticism*, New York, (1974) p. 204.

presenting. The validity of this consideration needs to be my foremost concern.

My approach to this study has mainly relied on such a guidance as that described by H. Coombes when he praised and included passages from the 'excellent things about critics and criticism' that he believed are conveyed in the writings of D. H. Lawrence: 'Literary criticism can be no more than a reasoned account of the feeling produced upon the critic by the book he is criticizing. Criticism can never be a science: it is, in the first place, much too personal, and in the second, it is concerned with values that science ignores. The touch-stone is *emotion*, not reason. We judge a work of art by its effect on our sincere and vital emotions, and nothing else. All the critical twiddle-twaddle about style and form, all the pseudo-scientific classifying and analysing of books in an imitation-botanical fashion, is mere impertinence and most dull jargon ... A critic must be able to feel the impact of a work of art in all its complexity and its force.'[2]

Not surprisingly my allegorical theories have already brought about such adverse academic comments as: 'Never in a month of Sundays will you persuade me that the *Canterbury Tales* is a work of allegory!' Of course, none of us should

---

[2] Coombes, H., *Literature and Criticism*, Pelican Books, 1963. (p.8)

believe to have arrived at the sole level of interpretation regarding such a comprehensive and diverse work as the *CT*, and if I have occasionally conveyed that impression to others I now take this opportunity to apologise for having sometimes been spirited away by my enthusiasm for the allegorical matter as I moved through what seemed to be an initial complexity. If not to be now, perhaps sometime in the future a few others will come to understand that I could do nothing other than follow the reading I reasoned to have been led into by Chaucer himself; that is what I have gleaned from my studies into the various works of the one that I take to be the most philosophically gifted and poetical writer I have personally read in the English language. One that for the expressed sincerity of his subject matter, and for his literary skills, I regard to be worthy of the highest possible honour and praise. I feel myself greatly indebted to Chaucer for his having granted me such a vision of his wisdom and skills of communication. I believe it was Rene Descartes (1596-1650) that declared a belief that the reading of all good books is to acquire conversations with the finest minds to be found in the past centuries. This could certainly be considered true when we appraise Chaucer's work.

An allegorical work is an oblique form of dialogue that's designed to carry underlying meanings to be derived from what initially appears to be a direct presentation. A compositon in which a writer consistently implies something other than the actual surface descriptions he presents; but such a narrative that on our deeper considerations suggest the more hidden significances. It conveys and brings that implied sentence home to the mind with a greater force and effect than if its lesson had been carried directly. Whereas the surface level of such a work appeals to the eye by means of our delight on the reading of its skilful presentation; the implied 'sentence' of what the text 'implies' rather than what it actually tells us on the surface level contains the profounder moral meanings.

In his *General Prologue* Chaucer presents us with the necessary 'signs' or pointers to the hidden identities of the various pilgrims; the Pardoner puts such as this rather well in the prologue to his tale: 'For though I telle noght his proper name, / Men shal wel knowe that it is the same, / By signes, and by othere circumstances;'[3] (*Pro. PardT* 417-19) secondly, within the various *Tales* Chaucer designs such a set of 'circumstances' as enable us to grasp the work's figurative complexities; and from our greater understanding of these gain the deeper meanings that are to be associated with this portrayal of an imagined pilgrimage taking place

---

3. All textual quotations are taken from *The Riverside Chaucer*, Editor Larry D. Benson, Third Edition, 1987, Oxford University Press, 1987. Henceforth cited as *Riverside.*

between Cheapside in London and the martyr (Thomas Becket) shrine at Canterbury Cathedral.

The more apprehensive reader of my claimed allegorical readings may benefit from the following cautionary consideration to be found in the astute observation of Rosemary Woolf's essay: 'Many people nowadays acquire an early and excessive familiarity with the *General Prologue* to the *Canterbury Tales*, which later blunts their sharpness of perception. Since the *Prologue* is read at school, necessarily out of its literary-historical context, its methods of satire seem to have an inevitablility and rightness which preclude either surprise or analysis. This natural tendency to remain uncritically appreciative of the *Prologue* has been partly confirmed by various works of criticism which, thought admirable in many ways, effusively reiterate that "here is God's plenty:" they thus awaken an enthusiastic response to the vitality and variety of the characterization in the *Prologue*, at the cost of making the exact manner and tone of Chaucer's satire quite indistinct.'[4]

Although this is obviously not the only reading worthy of study within the work, I believe that the real-life historical drama underlying the above mentioned 'signs and circumstances' depicts that the work's main concern is the welfare of the

[4] Woolf, Rosemary, *Geoffrey Chaucer: A Critical Anthology*, Penguin Books, Editor J.A. Burrow, (p. 206) 1982.

commonwealth, and that this expresses Chaucer's disquiet over the quality and therefore the future dangers that threatened the security of society and Richard II's kingship. It follows from such an unfamiliar belief that my allegorical method of conveyance faces a sharp and steep uphill task in securing critical acceptance; especially from those authoritative scholars that will perhaps be reluctant to accept such a figurative reading as appears to threaten the primary good of the many hours of enjoyable study they themselves have already spent in their considerations of the above mentioned 'God's plenty.' Those vivid and extremely humourous aspects that are also present within the *Canterbury Tales*.

I will therefore attempt to establish that by such as the above mentioned 'signs and circumstances' this work informs us how the pilgrims are to be identified as personalities that would have been more readily recognisable to Chaucer's knowing contemporaries; and that from such an awareness comes our unlocking of their thoughts and actions by means of their behavioural patterns within the accompanying tales. Such interpretation of personal and the resultant social consequences as are highly relevant to our understanding of King Richard II's psychological deviations during the period of his reign. Such changes as explain to us how it came about that the young king's initially pleasing potential digressed into the brutal tyranny that marked so many of his final years on the throne.

In this study the initial encouragement of allegory I have appreciated and found to be the most useful has been J. Leslie Hotson's *Colfox Vs.Chauntecleer* (1924) essay.[5] Later the main assistance has come from D. W. Robertson's excellent book on medieval allegory.[6] Professor Hotson's essay on the *Nun's Priest's Tale* has been described as: 'Even from this bare summary, not altogether consistent ... the whole interpretation is extremely conjectural. Yet it deserves to be recorded ... among the ingenious attempts to find political or social allegory in Chaucer's poems.'[7] Being another such highly informative and the now widely accepted edition, the *Riverside Chaucer* presents us with a similar appraisal: 'Hotson's theory that the work is an allegorical representation of the duel between Mowbray and Bolingbroke in September of 1397 is now almost universally rejected.'[8] Correct as are both of the above learned comments, mainly because it bolstered my own

---

[5]Hotson, J. Leslie, *Col-fox Vs. Chauntecleer*, (PMLA 39: 762-81)
[6] Robertson, D. W., Jr. *A Preface to Chaucer*. Studies in Medieval Perspectives, London. OUP. (1962)
[7] Robinson, F. N., *The Complete Works of Geoffrey Chaucer, Second Edition, Oxford Paperbacks, p. 751.* Henceforth referred to as Complete Works.
[8]*Riverside, p.935.*

belief of a connection that I had previously drawn with the historically described murder of Thomas Duke of Gloucester at Calais in 1398 when forming my own figurative interpretation of the *Nun's Priest's Tale*, I found that Professor Hotson's essay provided me with a reassuring invitation to progress further through what had become the slightly opened door of my own investigation.

As my study of the *CT* increased the figurative patterns I was forming became less reliant on the opinions of the non-allegorical schools of criticism that are now considered to present the main levels of academic interest. My growing understanding of Chaucer's text indicated the probability that, but with many significant changes, such an unfolding historical undertone as Professor Hotson believed to have found in his reading of the *NPT* could be consistently established within the whole of the *CT*. For example, though not drawing identical political attachments to the individuals that he had placed in his essay on the *NPT*, I was finding further hints of contemporary figures and events being hidden beneath the surface levels of other tales. I now relied on what I considered to be the truth of the following guide: 'Though the modern reader finds some of his meanings obscure, we may be sure that they were clear to his contemporaries. We can draw no other conclusion from the evidence of his firm, compact style, and his unfailing choice of the right word. When Chaucer's meaning is not plain to us, the fault lies in our ignorance either of his speech and education or of the smaller and more interesting facts of his life and times. Often we are baffled by a passage which we feel contains more meaning or humour than we can get from it.'[9]

William Witherle Lawrence was another that produced such a significant comment as Professor Hotson's above observation: 'Chaucer astonishes us again and agains by his modernity. His humour, one is tempted to say, is like nothing else in the middle ages, and a sense of humour is a wonderful solvent of the barriers imposed by time. He is so great a poet, his human sympathy is so pervasive, his knowledge of mankind so profound, his personal attitude towards the reader so intimate, that one easily gets to feel that the secrets of his art may best be understood by entering into close communion with him and throwing distracting commentaries aside.'[10] He also quoted the following: 'William James once wrote that "the wisest of critics is an altering being, subject to the better insight of the morrow, and right at any moment, only 'up to date' and 'on the whole.'"(pp. 8-9)

---

[9] Hotson, p. 762.
[10] Lawrence, William Witherle, _Chaucer and the Canterbury Tales,_ Columbia University Press, New York and London. (1964) p.5.

Although it was later that I arrived at D. W. Robertson's book, its contents interested me into a closer consideration of the persistence of the moral and immoral opposites that he described to be found within medieval literature. Especially so those contraries of Charity (*caritas*) and Cupidity (*cupiditas*) forms of love: 'St. Augustine concludes, on the basis of this and other assertions like that in 1 Tim. 1. 5, that "Scripture teaches nothing but charity nor condemns anything except cupidity." A discipline is thus afforded for the exegete. Those passages which promote charity or condemn cupidity are to be left with their literal significance; but all figurative interpretations must promote the love of God and of one's neighbour. If they do not, the interpreter is either decieved or deceiving, and the interpretations ar false.'[11] It was this described form of spiritual *caritas*, a charitable loving that directed mankind towards God; the opposite being *cupiditas*, a sensual form of love motivated by sensuality and the sin of self-pride, that ensured my growing understanding of the many mysteries I was finding to be implied within my earlier readings of the *Canterbury Tales*.

    A. Leigh DeNeef's excellent essay on *Robertson and the Critics* presents an informative clarification of Professor Robertson's approach to

---

[11] Robertson, p.295.

medieval literature: 'Risking a certain degree of over-simplification, we may say that one of the most significant features of the Middle Ages, as Robertson sees them, is a pervasive theological basis of life, fostered chiefly by the dominance of the Church. For the historical critic this matter is of enormous value, for it suggests that certain doctrines remained constant: "The common heritage of every civilized individual for more than a thousand years of European history." And as we shall see, the most significant of these doctrines is that of *caritas*, the love of neighbour and God. But even more important for Robertson's critical theory is the position of the Bible in this church-centred civilization: all theological activity centered on the study of Scripture; in fact, the ultimate purpose of *all* kinds of study was either the intepretation of the Sacred Text or the application of the principles which it contains.'[12]

Professor Hardison put the difficulties of deciphering such implications as are found in allegories rather well when he cited Boccaccio on them: 'The function of poets is to write, not to "rip up and lay bare the meaning which lies hidden in his inventions." In the *Life of Dante* Boccaccio remarked that "Anything gained with fatigue seems sweeter than what is understood without effort. The

---

[12]DeNeef, A. Leigh., *Robertson and the Critics*, Chaucer Review 2, (1967-8). p. 207.

plain truth, since it is understood easily, delights us and passes from the mind. But, in order that it may be more pleasing because acquired with labour, and therefore better valued, the poets hide the truth beneath things appearing quite contrary to it."'[13] I personally would add to this the possibility that they occasionally may have also hidden the truth in order to protect themselves from physical danger. Hardison also adds Boccaccio's guidance to all that approach such cryptical works: 'But I repeat my advice to those who would appreciate poetry, and unwind its difficult involutions. You must read, you must persevere, you must sit up nights, and you must inquire, and exert the utmost power of your mind. If one way does not lead to the desired meaning, take another; if obstacles arise, then still another; until, if your strength holds out, you will find that clear which at first looked dark.'[14]

Probably our greatest appreciation of the *CT* should be that its implied messages of contemporary history are worthy to be considered as a vehicle of future instruction to all present and future possessors of political power; especially so for those that tyrannically attempt to oppress their subjects. Here on the deeper allegorical level of our reading, we find a connecting stream of historical complements that imply Chaucer's increasing

---

[13] Hardison, p.191.
[14] Ibid. p. 208.

16

concerns over the despotic direction of the readily flattered King Richard II's reign. The implied history contained within these *Tales* informs us on both the psychological and on the social levels. They effectively and superbly describe why the peace of this king's reign came to be so often disturbed by those reckless policies he allowed to take place, and sometimes even encouraged to be taken against the social interests of his subjects.

The Chaucer that I have become familiar with, and will attempt to convey to my readers is the much loved and greatly admired poet of his contemporaries. My purpose will therefore be to trace how his constant application of the dialectical system of resolving psychological contradictions; even when these exist between direct opposities within the same personality, are portrayed to be taking place as a conflict within the framework of the above mentioned *caritas* and *cupiditas* forms of loving. That is we are here encouraged to evaluate the personal changes taking place within various artistically drawn 'aspects' or 'dispositions' of mind possessed by those that Chaucer presented as being the 'nyne and twenty in a compaignye / Of sondry folk' gathered 'in Southwerk at the Tabard.'

Assisted by such a growing understanding we readily come to comprehend the motivations and changing personalities of those contemporary individuals he implied to be on this pilgrimage.

Throughout my interpretations of such partly hidden, yet highly significant 'signs and circumstances,' I will attempt to confirm for the reader how this artistically drawn pilgrimage towards Canterbury provides us with Chaucer's closely observed and interlocking record of an increasingly turbulent piece of English history. I will endeavour to make it unambiguous that the allegorical narrative being presented implies the historical period from a time following King Richard's enthronement in 1377 to his forced abdication in 1399.

From my belief in the *CT*'s figurative composition it follows that I cannot accept that most of today's literal explanatory notes on the *CT* delve deep enough into the text to present us with the work's more crucial moral messages and interesting history. If unconcerned to investigate such carefully constructed allegorical indicators our awareness will allow us no more than resolutions of the surface 'chaff' which, however well and delightfully portrayed, conveys a far less significant level of understanding: "'Nay," quod the fox, "but God yeve hym meschaunce, / That is so undiscreet of governaunce / That jangleth whan he sholde holde his pees." Lo, swich it is for to be recchelees / And necligent, and truste on flaterye. / But ye that holden this tale a folye, / As of a fox, or of a cok and hen, / Taketh the moralite, goode men. / For

Seint Paul seith that al that written is, / To oure doctrine it is ywrite, ywis; / Taketh the fruyt, and lat the chaf be stille.' (*NPT* 3433-43)

By presenting such a figurative reading as I propose, one that links the pilgrims and their tales in such a way as does not appear to me to have previously been sufficiently considered by modern scholars; hopefully, this investigation may in time be taken to be both credible and highly important in both the literary and the historical levels: 'What appears to most of us to be "irrational" in scriptural allegory seemed to late antique and medieval Christians to be a reasonable and intellectually satisfying elaboration of the philosophy of the New Testament. At the same time, to those who wished earnestly for charity in their hearts nothing could have been more emotionally satisfying than the discovery of principles encouraging charity beneath the somewhat perplexing surfaces of Old Testament texts. The satisfactions of spiritual exegesis were both intellectually and emotionally very genuine, and they were closely assoiciated with the development of faith in the mind. The fact that scientific rationalism and romantic emotionalism seek very different ends should not cause us to close our minds, at least in an historical sense, to the possibilities for fulfilment which allegory offered to our Christian forefathers.'[15]

If this figurative presentation I give of King Richard II's behaviour is not conclusively found to be supported by a consistent and meaningful tie-in with the known facts of the king's personality and history; inevitably, and deservedly so it will not be acceptable to the reader. The task before me must therefore be one of introducing a very different but a nevertheless convincing interpretation to what has preceded on the *CT*; such a study as at the very least is shown to be worthy of serious consideration when it's compared with our present readings of the work. Not having fully taken on board the above mentioned difficulties to be faced by allegorical readers before their arrival at Boccaccio's 'the desired meanings;' in my opinion, most of the present critics have too readily cautioned us against even attempting to compose allegorical formations out of this work.

The consensus of critics have certainly been very dismissive of such as Hotson and Robertson, that sought to present a deeper understanding of the medieval literary traditions: 'Chaucer would have relished the irony that six hundred years after his birth a coterie of critics would arise, in a continent undiscovered in his day, who would apply these

---

[15] Robertson, p. 295.

very principles to the interpretation of his own works, and who would be prepared to demonstrate that his poems mean the very opposite of what they purport to say.'[16] Surely, such intelligent readers as Hotson and Robertson did not intend the 'very opposite' in their allegorical appraisals what we tend to find in their investigations is an exploration into that which they have considered to be a deeper and fuller understanding of what Chaucer 'purports to say.'

If such worthy critics as they succeeded in opening further the door to figurative investigation; then, those of us not previously aware of the possible intricacies of allegory should be happy to applaud their efforts, and to the very best of our abilities, at least seriously attempt to consider the journey they have took down those traditionally favoured pathways. If so decided in their dismissal regarding the possibility of such as an allegorical *CT*, it surely cannot be credible to determine exactly what it was that these earlier philosophical poets sought to convey. It's far more likely that Chaucer would have 'relished the irony' that over six centuries later so many of the foremost researchers into his work remain steadfast in their belief that his *Canterbury Tales* contains no significant allegorical levels.

---

[16] Bishop, Ian, *The Narrative Art of the Canterbury Tales*, Everyman's Library, London, (1988), p. 169.

Professor Robertson explained this matter of a deeper reading rather well in the following: 'As Hugh of St. Victor explains in the *Didascalicon*, the exposition of a text involves the examination of three things: the *letter*, the *sense*, and the *sentence*. A study of the lettter involves the techniques of grammatical analysis. The sense is the obvious or surface meaning of a text, and the *sentence* is its doctrinal content or "higher" meaning. All texts, by virtue of the fact that they are texts, have a letter to be studied; some have letter and sense alone; some, which are meaningless without interpretation, have only letter and sentence; and some have all three. The purpose of exposition is to arrive at the *sentence*, since a text which has no third level does not require explanation. Following this convention, it became customary after the twelfth century to speak of the import of a text, whether sacred or profance, as its *sentence*.'[17]

Dante compared allegory to a hidden truth under the cloak of fables; a truth hidden beneath a beautiful and meaningful fiction. In 1598 we find that Francis Thynne wrote the following intriguing comment: 'In one open parliamente (as I have herde John Thynne reporte, being then a member of the howse) when talke was had of Bookes to be forbidden, Chaucer had there for euer byn

---

[17] Robertson, p. 315.

condemned, had yt not byn that his woorkes had byn counted but fables.'[18] From such as the above observations my reading of the *CT* as a series of allegories relies on a constant and deeper awareness of descriptions that can readily be translated into our better understanding of the main real-life characters and of their history. When so interpreted these 'dispositions' or 'aspects' of the significant personalities readily demonstrate the consistency of Chaucer's figurative intentions throughout his *Canterbury Tales*.

Six hundred and more years have now passed since Chaucer's death, and so we should surely turn away from those generally held beliefs that the *CT* display no interest in the reckless and calamitous politics of King Richard II's reign. Instead of such a shallow appraisal of his work we should attempt to understand how bravely, and that in such a brutal and tyrannous time, he expressed his astute observations on such serious matters as his sovereign's too readily a listening to those influential false flatterers that thronged his court.

Such criticisms of the king as I propose to argue for here should not be considered inconceivable within the allegorical tradition. Barbara Tuchman informs us that 'Denouncing the

---

[18] Thynne, Francis, *Animadversions,* Now Newly Edited from the MS. in the Bridgewater Library by G. H. Kingsley, M.D., London. MDCCCLXV. (p.7.)

age for decadence was in fashion, but the decadence was felt as real, and the sense of a moral decline from some better day in the past was insistent. The poets wrote for the very circles they denounced and they must have touched some responsive chord. Deschamps - who never left off scolding - was made chamberlin to Louis d'Orleans in 1382.'[19] J. A. Burrow is another that has explained this matter of poetic licence with a greater weight of scholarship than I could hope to express: 'Twelfth-century France and fourteenth-century Italy, in particular, furnish evidence of a loftier view of the poet - something like the humanists' Neoplatonic view of the poet as an inspired seer, expressing profound truths is his fables ... In practice even Neoplatonic criticism in the Middle Ages tended to decode poetic allegories into plain statements of moral, cosmological, or historical truth - statements which were not themselves in any sense fictive.'[20]

My hope is that this study will serve as a significant extension to the efforts presented by the above mentioned Hotson and Robertson; those that I believe held a worthy and capable understanding of the medieval literary tradition. Should I succeed in this objective other readers may then become as

---

[19] Tuchman, Barbara W. '*A Distant Mirror. The Calamitous 14th Century*.' Penguin Books, 1980. (p. 509)
[20] Burrow, J.A., <u>Medieval Writers and Their Work, Middle English Literature and its Background 1100-1500</u>. Oxford Univesity Press, (p. 16) 1982.

interested by what I have written as I have by the efforts of others such as Hotson and Robertson. They may also experience the inspiration and pleasure that encouraged me in this attempt to pursue a further unfolding of the *Canterbury Tales*. Of course, many more undetected historical parallels exist than those I will have but lightly touched upon in the following pages. My primary objective and hope being that what I present here will interest others enough to develop the greater weight of their scholarship into this small lot of my allegorical readings.

The History

The English feudal system of government readily accepted the king's role to be that of a divinely ordained symbol of national unity. Being the country's leading lord the king personified social justice and with this the God-approved position of sovereign power. On becoming sovereign he was sworn and expected to represent his primary role of being a just keeper of the traditionally held social order. Literary descriptions of kingship tend to praise a good and strong ruler who governs his kingdom well or they condemn a weak and brutal tyrant that tears it to pieces. Despotic oppression by excessive taxation, or by such unlawful actions as confiscation of a subject's property, undermined the security of the body politic; then, regardless of his being considered as God's anointed ruler, such actions endangered a sovereign's reign and along with this his personal safety.

The coronation oaths of 'Fealty and Acceptance' that were given and accepted at the coronations of English sovereigns in the 14th century disclose how far Richard II transgressed from the main demands required of his behaviour: 'The Archbishop of Canterbury shall oppose and ask the king the same day if he will hold and guarantee and keep the laws and the customs granted to his people of old by devout and rightwise kings beforehand. Also, if he will swear it, in particular the laws and customs and the liberties of the glorious King Edward to the people and the clergy. And the king shall behold that he will keep all these forsaid things. Then shall the Archbishop show and declare certain articles to which the king shall swear:

The first point: "Thou shall keep full peace and accord in God and to the Church to the people and to the clergy." And the king shall swear. "I shall do."

The second point: "Thou shall keep in all these domains rightful and every rightwiseness and discretion with mercy and truth." And the king shall swear, "I shall do."

The third point: "Grant thou all rightful laws and customs to behold and that thou wilt defend and strengthen them to that worship if God to his might and powers which shall choose." And the the king shall answer, "I grant and behold it."[21]

Heredity sequence was itself upheld in the sovereign's keeping of the above mentioned coronation oaths to protect the traditional laws. This matter is put rather well in the *Canterbury Tales* when the Monk draws a comparison between the behaviour of Nebuchadnezzar and that of his son

---

[21] Online: http:/ www.dragonbear.com/fealty.html.

Belshazzar. The father being a sovereign who eventually regretted his previous misbehaviour and 'Thanked God, and evere his lyf in feere / Was he to doon amys or moore trespace; / And til that tyme he leyd was on his beere / He knew that God was ful of myght and grace. / His sone, which that highte Balthasar, / That heeld the regne after his fader day, / He by his fader koude noght be war, / For proud he was of herte and of array, / And eek an ydolastre was he ay. / His hye estaat assured hym in pryde; / But Fortune caste hym doun, and ther he lay, / And sodeynly his regne gan divide.' (*MkT* 2179-2190)

The first of King Richard's two wives, the country's much loved Queen Anne died in 1394. Following her death and increasingly so subsequent to his second marriage in 1396 to Isabel of Valois, his French child bride, the king's previously partly restrained imperious tendencies came to the fore and seem to have encouraged him into the final disastrous phase of his tyranny. Here in the *Canterbury Tales* we find that Chaucer provides us with what I take to be an unbiased account of King Richard's reckless personality; and especially of those final disastrous policies that eventually led to his forced abdication. Not only does the work personify Richard's fluctuations between moods of high merriment and terrifying anger towards others, it also presents us with Chaucer's opinions how these came about and why they should be considered so dominant a factor when we come to appraise his eventual dethronement.

The consensus of today's scholars tend to see the *CT* as being the work of a poet who 'wisely' ignored the turbulent politics of his day. Such a low dopinion contradicts those of his contemporaries. As Jeanne E. Krochalis has noted, when the poet Hoccleve cautioned Prince Henry to heed the advice of wise counsellors he did so by drawing a comparison between Chaucer's prowess in such matters, and by doing he stated his own deficiencies:

> To God your herte bowe
> If yee desire men hir hertes bende
> To yow. What kyng nat dredith God offende
> Ne nat rekkith do him disobeissance,
> He shal be disobeyed eek, par chance.
> The first fyndere of our fair langage,
> Hath seid, in cas semblable, and othir mo,
> So hyly wel that it is my dotage
> For to expresse or touche any of tho.[22]

Not having understood Chaucer's allegories, she naturally finds Hoccleve's positioning of the above Chaucer reference in *The Regement of*

[22] Krochalis, Jeanne E., *Hoccleve's Chaucer Portrait,* The Chaucer Review, Vol. 21, No. 2. (1986), p. 240. Pennsylvania State University Press.

Princes to be problematic: 'The *Regement* is dedicated to the future Henry V, and the praise of Chaucer is embedded in a section stressing the ruler's need for good counsellors ... The placement of the Chaucer passage in the *Regement* as a whole is curious. Hoccleve has just spent about a hundred lines urging Henry to heed good councellors; kings need counsellors as horses need bridles. The king who dares to disobey God will be disobeyed in his turn. And this is the sentiment Hoccleve ascribes to Chaucer, who "Hath seyde in caas semblable and other moo / So hyly well." Of what Chaucerian work is Hoccleve thinking here?'[23]

On June 21, 1377, Richard's enthronement had been accompanied by an impressive display of social acceptance; on Michaelmas Day, September 29, 1399, his reign ended in circumstances far removed from this well received commencement:

> I not what you eylid but if it ese were;
> For first a youre anoyntynge alle were
> youre owen,
> Bothe hertis and hyndis and helde
> of non other;
> Ne lede of youre lond but as a liege aughte,
> Tyl ye, of youre dulnesse deseueraunce
> made,

---

[23] Ibid., p, 240.

Thoru youre side signes that shente all the
browet,
And cast adoun the crokk the colys amyd.'[24]

The above lines contain two important
pointers; firstly, that the traditional feudal display of
loyalty granted to a new sovereign had been readily
extended to this young king at his coronation: 'Alle
were youre owen;' secondly, a hint that Richard's
love of ('ese') could have been the spark that
generated the increasing social hatred of his reign.
The historically recorded extravagances at his court
appear to have been accompanied by his complete
disregard for the welfare of his subjects, and such
behaviour eventually played a significant part in the
civil rebellion against his rule. Not only was the
flattering influence of his 'cursid conceill' to blame
in his eventual downfall; he himself was also
considered responsible for the 'pillynge of youre
peple youre prynces to plese.'[25]

As this term 'prynces' could have indicated
his second wife, the anonymous poet of this poem
may well be inferring that Richard's 'tallage of
youre townnes without ony were'[26] had been partly
raised in order to present his young queen with a

---

[24] The Piers Plowman Tradition, ed. Helen Barr, (Everyman's Library) ,
Passus II, 46-52, (p.110).
[25] Ibid., Passus 1. l. 100.
[26] Ibid., Passus l. L, 102.

constant flow of extravagant gifts: 'Richard appears to have treated the young Isabel as the child that he never had. He indulged her various whims and fancies, and at Christmas and other festivals he showered her with presents ... She and her entourage became an object of social criticism.'[27] There were many of political importance that considered Queen Isabel's presence in England to have been an adverse influence on the country's stability: 'Concerning her departure, of which I was witness ... those in power chafed, some cursing her coming into this land as being the cause of all its troubles.'[28]

In 1386-88, an earlier period of the reign, the king's uncle, the later murdered Duke of Gloucester, had been the leading member of the group of nobles that sought to contain Richard's most dangerous excesses. The Appellant Council as they were known denounced as traitors and executed those they considered to be exercising the greatest treasonable influence on the young king's behaviour. Completely disregarding the earlier sworn oaths of forgiveness he had granted to these same appellants; in 1397 Richard successfully overpowered them and claimed they had previously undermined his royal prerogative. Thomas of Gloucester was proclaimed to have been a traitor

[27] Saul, Nigel, _Richard II,_ Yale University Press, 1997, (p. 457).
[28] _Chronicon Adam de Usk A.D. 1377-1421_ Oxford, 1904, (p. 229).

and following his murder at Calais, his properties and those of the other former appellants were annexed into the royal treasury and shared amongst the king and his allies.

Perilous as such behaviour was to the stability of his reign, and with this to his own personal safety, it was not the breaking of the sacred oath of forgiveness to Gloucester, but his later disinheriting of the popular Henry Bolingbroke that provided Richard's subjects with a powerful and capable leader for the desired social uprising against his misgovernment of the realm. Heir to the vast Lancasterian estates, Henry had previously been promised his traditional legal inheritance at the death of his father. Following John of Gaunt's death the reckless Richard extended the years of his cousin's unjust exile to a life sentence, and he even went so far as to confiscate his vast Lancastrian properties. Such an act of tyranny determined Henry's decision to disobey his term of banishment and his return to England resulted in his necessary dethronement of the king.

Considering John of Gaunt's steadfast support of Richard in those former times of his political troubles, such a severe treatment of his son was an unbelievably foolish act. In Shakespeare's mention of the event we find the Duke of York, another of the king's uncles, confronting his nephew with a plea that he considers both the injustice and the possible consequences of such an action:

> Take Hereford's right away, and take
> from Time
> His charters and his customary rights;
> Let not to-morrow, then ensue to-day;
> Be not thyself, - for how art thou a king
> But by fair sequence and succession?
> Now, afore God - God forbid I say true -
> If you do wrongfully seize Hereford's rights,
> Call in the letters-patents that he hath
> By his attorney-general to sue
> His livery and deny his offered homage,
> You pluck a thousand dangers on your head,
> You lose a thousand well-disposed hearts,
> And prick my tender patience to those
> thoughts
> Which honour and allegiance cannot think.[29]

The prideful and easily flattered king ignored that the oaths binding him to his subjects relied on the strength of their mutual acts of support within the feudal alliance. He failed to consider that his unjust dismemberment of the Lancastrian estates also unlawfully disinherited Henry's family. Such an outrage against the traditional rights of the

---

[29] *The Complete Works of William Shakespeare*, Richard II, Act 2, Sc. i, ll.196-209. Editor W, J. Craig, Oxford , (1947)

House of Lancaster would inevitably be opposed by whatever means Henry possessed to regain his lawful properties.

Furthermore it followed that if Richard was allowed to confiscate the lands of such a leading and true member of his own royal family; such an act of tyranny threatend the established hereditary sequence of all those lords within the realm that refused him in any of his future requests. It should have been very obvious to him that Henry would not be without military support in whatever response he decided upon in order to regain his legal feudal inheritance: 'News of Richard's decision determined Lancaster to return at the first opportunity. On 29 of May Richard left for Ireland, leaving the Duke of York as Regent in England. On 4 July Lancaster landed at Ravenspur, and was rapidly joined by the northern lords. They marched on Bristol and before the end of July the Regent had abandoned resistance. Richard landed in Wales before the end of that month but became discouraged, and fled to the North, where he remained until his submission to Lancaster on 19th August.'[30]

Thereafter the political events quickly developed: 'After the King had spoken apart with the said Duke (Henry) and the Archbishop, looking

---

[30] Hughes, Dorothy, *Illustrations of Chaucer's England*, Rolls of Parliament, *Translated from the Latin,* London, 1918, (p. 286)

from one to the other with a cheerful countenance, as it seemed to those standing round, calling all those present to him, he said openly before them that he was ready to make renunciation and resignation according to his promise. And although, to avoid the labour of such lengthy reading, he might, as he was told, have read the renunciation (that was contained in a parchment schedule) by deputy, the King, holding the schedule in his hand said at once willingly, as it seemed, and with cheerful looks, that he would read it himself. And he read it through distinctly, absolving his lieges, and making renunciation, oath, and declaration, as is fully contained in the said schedule, and signed it with his own hand.'[31]   Thereby Henry declared himself to be the legitimate heir to the throne, and he was crowned King Henry IV.

The following short poem is mistakenly taken to be Chaucer's only censure of Richard's despotism:

---

[31] Ibid., pp.287-88

36

Lak of Stedfastnesse

Somtyme the world was so stedfast
and stable
That mannes word was obligacioun,
And now it is so fals and decevable
That word and deed, as in conclusioun,
Ben nothing lyk, for turned up-so-doun
Is al this world for mede and wilfulnesse,
That al is lost for lak of stedfastnesse.

What maketh this world to be so variable
But lust that folk have in dissensioun?
For among us now a man is holde unable
But if he can, by som collusioun,
Don his neighbour wrong or oppressioun.
What causeth this but wilful wrecchedness,
That al is lost for lak of stedfastnesse.

Truthe is put doun, resoun is holden fable;
Vertu hath now no dominacioun;
Pitee exyled, no man is merciable;
Through covetyse is blent discrecioun.
The world hath mad a permutacioun
Fro right to wrong, fro trouthe to fikelnesse,
That al is lost for lak of stedfastnesse.

Lenvoy to King Richard

O prince, desyre to be honourable,
Cherish thy folk and hate extorcioun!
Suffre nothing that may be reprevable
To thyn estate don in thy regioun.
Shew forth thy swerd of castigacioun,
Dred God, do law, love trouthe
and   worthinesse,
And wed thy folk agein to stedfastnesse.

(Riverside, p. 654)

The above 'permutacioun / From right to wrong;' and with it the implied castigation of Richard's failure to 'dred God, do law, love trouthe and worthinesse,' indicates that it was no mere chance fall from Fortune's favour but rather his constant acts of tyranny that led to this king's dethronement. As would have other perceptive contemporaries; Chaucer had earlier understood the likely consequence of the social disenchantment brought about by the increasing tyranny.

There are many examples to be found within his work that testify his belief that the prophet kings were the highest examples of a just rule. Richard's policies had transgressed far from the necessary charity of Christian love that the sovereign lord required to display towards his subjects; and those kings that abandoned God's Eternal Laws also disregarded the good of temporal laws: 'For smoothly the lawe of God is the love of God; for which David the prophete seith: "I have loved thy lawe, and hated wikkednesse and hate;" he that loveth God kepeth his lawe and his word.' (*ParsT* 125) 'Homycide is eek in yevynge of wikked conseil by fraude, as for to yeven conseil to areysen wrongful custumes and taillages. / Of whiche seith Salomon: "leon rorynge and bere hungry been like to the crueel lordships in withholding or abreggynge of the shepe (or the hyre), or in withdrawynge of the almesse of povre folk."' (*ParsT* 567 -68)

Faithfulness to God's requested love towards their subjects presented rulers with their greatest personal safety: 'Tullius seith, "Ther nys no myght so gret of any emperour that longe may endure, but he have moore love of the peple than drede."' (*Mel* 1192) Chaucer's figure of the Parson also declares this matter in the following manner: 'Thynk eek that of swich seed as cherles spryngen, of swich seed spryngen lordes. As wel may the cherl be saved as the lord. / The same deeth that taketh the cherl, swich deeth taketh the lord. Wherfore I rede, do right so with thy cherl, as thou woldest that thy lord dide with thee, if thou were in his plit. / I rede thee, certes, that thou, lord, were in swich wise with thy cherles that they rather love thee than drede. / I woot wel ther is degree above degree, as reson is, and skile is that men do hir devoir ther as it is due, but certes, extorcions and despit of your underlynges is dampnable.' (*ParsT* 761-64)

Nothing could possibly have held greater relevance as being wise counselling of a king than the following passage on the limitation of kingly power: 'The Pope calleth hymself servant of the servantz of God; but for as muche as the estaat of hooly chirche ne myght nat han be, ne the commune profit myghte nat han be kept, ne pees and rest in erthe, but if God hadde ordeyned that som men hadde hyer degree and som men lower, / therfore was sovereyntee ordeyned, to kepe and mayntene and deffenden hire underlynges or hire subgetz in resoun, as ferforth as it lith in hire powere, and nat to destroyen hem ne confounde. / Wherfore I seye that thilke lordes that been lyk wolves, that devouren the possessiouns or the catel of povre folk wrongfully, withouten mercy or mesure, / they shul receyven by the same mesure that they han mesured to povre folk the mercy of Jhesu Crist, but if it be amended.' (*ParsT* 773-76)

General Prologue

The *General Prologue*'s allegorical structure adopts a system of psychological opposites between contrasting representations of individuals as a means of investigating those three real-life persons that Chaucer personifies here to be various dispositions of himself; of King Richard II and of Queen Isabel, Richard's second wife. By means of such a manner of presentations we are led into the *Tales* themselves through a method of investigation that provides an exciting and highly informative way of getting to know each individual from an examination of the differing 'aspects' of character possessed by each representative portrayal.

At the start of the pilgrimage 'Wel nyne and twenty in a compaignye' (*GP* 24) gather under 'the yonge sonne;' (*GP* 7) in the work's final prologue the setting sun has 'descended / So lowe that he nas nat, to my sighte, / Degrees nyne and twenty as in highte.' (*ParsT* 2-4) This later recall of 'nyne and twenty' degrees implying the sun to be setting on the history of the three persons previously portrayed as being the 'twenty nine' dispositions or aspects of those that have been presented within the *Canterbury Tales*. Chaucer, by such a method of dissecting his chosen pilgrims, sought to present his readers with a fuller insight into the personalities of the three being investigated.

In order to understand this lengthy work of allegory it follows that we initially need to be able to recognise the 'signs' that link each pilgrim with their real-life counterpart. Thereafter we should be the more able to assess the personality changes taking place within each character as they 'pilgrimmage' through this artistic portrayal that eventually causes us to consider the conclusions to be drawn out of the individual descriptions and their tales.

(Chaucer / the Narrator)

The Narrator is readily identified outside the work's allegorical framework. In the *Prologue to Sir Thopas* we find the following: *Bihoold the murye wordes of the Hoost to Chaucer*: 'Whan seyd was al this miracle, every man / As sobre was that wonder was to se, / Til that oure Hooste japen tho bigan, / And thanne at erst he looked upon me, / And seyde thus: "What man artow?" quod he; / "Thou lookest as thou woldest fynde an hare, / For evere upon the ground I se thee stare. / Approche neer, and looke up murily."' (*Thop.* 691-98) Following this command we have the following introduction: '*Heere bigynneth Chaucer's Tale of Thopas.*' Such a form of Chaucer's identification also appears at the close of his tale: '*Heere is ended Chaucers Tale of Melibee and of Dame Prudence.*'

He is also identified as the Clerk in that tale's *Lenvoy de Chaucer*. I will present more on this matter when the tale's allegory is detailed and the identifying envoy's relevance to the underlying history is closely examined. The significance here being that multiple representatives of Chaucer can be found outside as well as inside of the *CT*'s allegorical structure: both the Narrator and the Clerk are seen to identify the same real-life figure of Chaucer.

The Narrator disposition describes himself to be an obtuse personality: 'My wit is short, ye may wel understonde.' (*GP* 746) A cautioning that this self-disparaging is not a true reflection of the intended reality being depicted has been presented when the Narrator not only affirms his reliance on the highest of learned authorities, but also states that his purpose is the correction of those whose bad behaviour justifies condemnation: 'Whoso shal telle a tale after a man, / He moot reherce as ny as ever he kan / Everich a word, if it be in his charge / Al speke he never so rudeliche and large, / Or ellis he moot telle his tale untrewe, / Or feyne thyng, or fynde wordes newe. / He may nat spare, although he were his brother;' (*GP* 731-37) 'For Catoun seith that he that gilty is / Demeth alle thing be spoke of hym, ywis.' (*Pro CYT* 688-89) 'Eek Plato seith, whoso that kan hym rede, / The wordes moost be cosyn to the dede.' (*GP* 741-42)

(King Richard / the Host)

Although the Host is not one of the 'nyne and twenty in a compaignye / Of sondry folk, by aventure yfalle / In felaweshipe, and pilgrims were they alle, / That toward Caunterbury wolden ryde;' (*GP* 24-27) his constant interruptions and 'merry' presence throughout the *Canterbury Tales* justifies his identification within the group. I consider the Host to be as true a representation as we will probably ever find of King Richard II: 'A semely man oure Hooste was withalle / For to han been a marchal in an halle. / A large man he was with eyen stepe – / A fairer burgeys is ther noon in Chepe – / Boold of his speche, and wys, and wel ytaught, / And of manhood lakkede right naught. / Eek therto he was right a myrie man.' (*GP* 751-57) Calculated to be at least six feet tall from a measurement of his bones in 1871, King Richard could certainly be described as a large man.

The many indicators of the Host's 'jollity' suggest that these observations were unlikely to have been inserted without such a disposition being prominent in his personality: 'I saugh nat this yeer so myrie a compaigny;' (*GP* 764) 'Fayn wolde I doon you myrthe, wiste I how. / And of a myrthe I am right now bythought.' (*GP* 766-67) 'But ye be myrie, I wol yeve yow myn heed!' (*GP* 782)

Shakespeare's description of King Richard also indicates him to possess a 'skipping' temperament:

> The skipping King, he ambled up and down,
> With shallow jesters, and rash bavin wits,
> Soon kindled and soon burnt, carded
> his state,
> Mingled his royalty with capering fools,
> Had his great name profaned with
> their scorns,
> And gave his countenance against his name
> To laugh at gibing boys, and stand the push
> Of every beardless vain comparative.[32]

When we have become familiar with Chaucer's cryptical creation of words that assist the development of his themes; especially so those that contain relevant identifying significances, we become aware why this Host figure has been named Harry Bailly. 'Harry' (Eng. Harry from Anglo-Saxon '*hergian*,') that is to plunder or lay waste: 'And haryed forth by arme, foot, and too;' (*KnT* 2726) that is a name that could be taken to imply King Richard's social 'plundering' of his subjects; the surname 'Bailly' hints the presence of a bailiff, a collector of taxes for his lord. In the final years of the reign, the likely time when the last strands of the

---

[32] Shakespeare, King Henry IV, Part One, Act III, sc., ii, lines 60-67.

45

General Prologue were being gathered, the 'plundering bailly' would then have been a very apt pointer to this hidden presence. The *Friar's Tale*, a tale that constantly implies Richard's economic harshness towards his subjects, yokes together a bailiff / Summoner with the devil / fiend: '"Now, brother," quod this somonour, "I yow preye, / Teche me, whil that we ryden by the weye, / Syn that ye been a baillif as am I / Som subtiltee, and tel me faithfully / In myn office how that I may moost wynne, / And spareth nat for conscience ne synne."' (*FriT* 1417-22)

Another hint of King Richard's tyrannical authority comes in the Host's announcement that all the pilgrims must immediately, and without debate, agree with his requests or pay for the pilgrimage: 'Hoold up youre hondes, withouten moore speche,' (*GP* 783) 'And whoso wole my juggement withseye / Shal paye al that we spenden by the weye.' (*GP* 805-06) When we become aware of the historical reality behind this representative figure we are not surprised that the pilgrims so readily comply with his demands: 'And we wol reuled been at his devys / In heigh and lough; and thus by oon assent / We been accorded to his juggement.' (*GP* 816-18) Thomas Tyrwhitt (1730-86), probably the first establisher of discerning studies into Chaucer's work, noted that the following phrase: 'In heigh and lough,' designated the opposites of sovereignty on

46

the one hand and the complete submission of subjects on the other.[33]

King Richard's marriage to Isabel of Valois in 1396 complemented his increasingly unlawful attacks on the traditional rights of his subjects. Not surprisingly therefore that the Host appears to be justifiably concerned his wife's influence on his behaviour could become detrimental to his safety: 'I woot wel she wol do me slee som day / Som neighebor, and thanne go my way; / For I am perilous with knyf in honde.' (*Pro MkT* 1917-19) Probably the lion's primacy in the order of animals, a lordship held to be emblematic of a sovereign's position in human society, underlies Harry Bailly's comparison of his own reckless behaviour with that of 'a wilde leoun, fool hardy.' (*ProMkT* 1916)

As the allegorical framework of this work unfolds it increasingly discloses the fullness of the historical dimensions. With this awareness comes our perception of Queen Isabel's implied presence behind the figure of Goode-lief; as we shall see later, this was a significant name to have given to the Host's fearsome wife: 'By Goddes bones, whan I bete my knaves, / She bryngeth me forth the grete clobbed staves, / And crieth, "Slee the dogges everichoon, / And brek hem, bothe bak and every boon!"' (*Pro MkT* 1897-1900) Harry's detail of her

[33] Tyrwhitt, Thomas , The Poetical Works of Geoffrey Chaucer, 1883, London,. (p. 178).

urging him into action against his 'knaves' will be seen to contrast the prudent counselling to be found in the *Melibee*, that tale's likely figurative representative of King Richard's first wife.

Queen Isabel's childhood increases the comic effect of the 'large' and 'manly' Host's expressed fear of her physical might: 'I dar nat hire withstonde, / For she is byg in armes, by my feith.' (*MkT* 1920-21) More on this later. Probably it's useful here to quote once again from Professor Hotson's essay on the *Nun's Priest's Tale*: 'Chaucer, of course, does point a moral at the end of his fable; yet I question whether the medieval reader, although delighted with the mock-heroics and pleased with the moral, was satisfied with the very general nature of the satire on human fraility in the rest of the tale. Moreover, the thing is told with such verve and high spirits, that it is hard not to suspect that author and audience saw something further in it to amuse them: something besides the main comic dialogue, the characters, and the stock situation, which time has hidden from us.'[34] Later in this book I will add extremely humourous Chaucer comments that directly relate to the above 'byg in armes' description.

---

[34] Hotson, pp. 763-764.

(Chaucer / the Knight)

Without presenting us with any conclusive evidence; today's critics appear too readily to assume Chaucer's birth to be of a later date than that presented by the earlier writers: 'Speght, in 1598, was the first biographer of Chaucer to suggest a date for his birth: "About the second or third year of Edward 3." The "Life" published in the edition of Chaucer's works edited by John Urry in 1721 attempts to make this specific: "In the second year of the reign of King Edward III., A.D. 1328." Although no positive authority was given or is known for this date, it became established as the traditional date of Chaucer's birth, and was used until increasing knowledge of Chaucer's life and writings in the nineteenth century showed that it was untenable. The abandonment of 1328 as the date of Chaucer's birth and the acceptance of a date between 1340 and 1345 came about only slowly.'[35] Although I much appreciate the helpfulness of the Crow and Olson researches in their compiling the *Life-Records*; nevertheless, I dispute that the 'increasing knowledge' they claim for 'the abandonment of 1328' regarding Chaucer's age holds any certainty.

---

[35] Crow and Olson, Chaucer Life-Records, Oxford, (pp.372-73), 1966.

Robert Bell has the following footnote: 'That Chaucer had attained a considerable age at the time of his death is placed beyond doubt by decisive testimonies. Gower, in 1392-3, speaks of him as "Now in his dayes old;" Occleve, lamenting his death, apostrophises him - "O maister deere and fadir reverent," terms which according to Sir Harris Nicolas were "long used to indicate respect for age, and for superiority in any pursuit of science ...." Leland says that he "lived to the period of grey hairs, and at length found old age his greatest disease." We recall the well-known portrait, painted by Occleve from memory (Harl. MS., 4866) agrees with these descriptions and presents Chaucer with white hair and beard; his features bearing evident traces of old age. In another portrait, found in an early, if not contemporary, copy of Occleve's poems in the Royal MS., 17, D. vi., he also appears very old, holding, as in Occleve's portrait, a string of beads in his left hand.'[36]

Other than a person whose life had been spent in a constant state of physical toil, it's difficult to accept such an aged appearance in one now claimed to have been around his mid or late fifties at the time of his death. Hoccleve respected Chaucer far too much to have presented him appearing twenty and more years older than he

[36]Bell. Robert, Poetical Works of Geoffrey Chaucer. Vol. 1. (10-11) London, Charles Grifins and Co., Stationary Hall Court. (n.d.)

really looked. We need here to recall Professor Manly's opinion when he comments on the subject of Chaucer's career: 'It may be freely admitted that all these new views concerning Chaucer's career are speculative, but it should be borne in mind that most of the current views are no less speculative, and that even if no certain conclusions can be reached, it is worth while to prevent speculation from hardening into accepted teachings.'[37] I believe that this argument is definitely to be reflected upon when we come to regard the modern dating of Chaucer's age.

Professor Manly arrived at incorrect conclusions when he attempted to identify the pilgrims outside an allegorical framework: 'Of all the studies tending to show that in painting the portraits of the Canterbury pilgrims Chaucer worked from living models, the earliest was perhaps the study of the Knight which I read before the American Philological Association in 1908 under the title "A Knight Ther Was." The evidence produced did not, to be sure, result in the disclosure of a single individual of whom it could be asserted with confidence that he was the original of the portrait of the Knight, but rather in establishing the fact that the career ascribed to the Knight was a possible and natural career and was illustrated even

---

[37] Manly, John Matthews, *Some New Light On Chaucer,* New York, (1951), p.67.

in minute detail by knights belonging to a family whose members were well known to Chaucer and were well-known figures of the day.

In making that study I have set forth with the assumption that if the Knight were a realistic portrait of one recognizable by Chaucer's readers, the original would certainly be a conspicuous figure of the time. Furthermore, it seemed highly probable that if he were such a person, he would have been called upon to testify in the famous controversy in 1386 between the Scrope and Grosvenor families over the coat of arms "asure, a bend or," which each of them claimed. I therefore carefully examined the careers of the knights who testified in that controversy, with the result just stated ... In these campaigns, which were among the most outstanding and picturesque events of the time, two members of the Scrope family - a family in whose behalf Chaucer himself testified - were prominent figures, and I suggested the possibility that the portrait might be a composite portrait of these two men.'[38]

Although I consider that Professor Manly arrived at the truth when stating his belief of the Knight being 'a realistic portrait recognizable by Chaucer's readers;' and that he was also correct when he noted the likelihood the Knight would have been called upon to testify in the 'famous

---

[38] Ibid. pp.254-255.

controversy in 1386;' although aware that Chaucer attended that parliament as a knight, and that he had also taken part in the above mentioned 'famous controversy;' due to his not having considered the allegorical form of these tales he failed to question the likelihood of Chaucer having identified himself as this knightly figure. Probably another significant guide to this identification comes in the comment that the Knight possessed a 'sovereyn prys;' (*GP* 67) in my opinion this is a direct allusion to the considerable 'price' of sixteen pounds ransom that on the 1st March, 1360, King Edward III had paid for Chaucer's release from the French wars.[39]

As had the Knight, in some capacity or other it seems very likely that Chaucer had also ridden at Satalye (1361), Alexandria (1365) and Leyes (1367). The archives of Navarre at Pamplona have been found to contain a note of safe-conduct that, between 22 February and Pentecost (24 May) 1366, was probably granted to Chaucer and three companions.[40] If this note of safe-conduct does indicate our Chaucer, such a well documented evidence of his passage through the lands of Charles II in 1366 places him close, and at the relevant times, to at least one of the above mentioned campaigns. However, the most telling evidence I am able to present of Chaucer being the

---

[39] Crow and Olson, *Chaucer Life-Records*, Oxford, 1966, (pp. 23-28).
[40] Ibid. (pp. 64-6).

reality behind this Knight will be explained later when the allegorical formations of the *CT* become more evident to the reader, and these linkages in turn are shown to alert us to the probable truth in my belief of this pilgrim's real-life identity.

When the *General Prologue* is considered within an allegorical format its figurative significance makes our understanding of the jousting descriptions the more acceptable: 'And foughten for oure feith at Tramyssene / In lystes thries, and ay slayn his foo.' (*GP* 62-63) The reading that this 'worthy' and 'wise' Knight was a mercenary, and that the true viciousness of his character is evidenced in his being described to have 'slayn' three opponents in the lists is then understood to require a reappraisal: 'Chaucer now adds one small detail which tells us more about the Knight's character than almost anything else. He tells us that every time the Knight has fought in the lists, he has killed his foe. Of course, from the way it is tossed in, it sounds like the final accolade. But is it? The whole spirit of the tournament lay in displaying skill, courage and generosity - not in killing your opponent. To be sure, the more skilful the jousters, the more liable they were to do each other serious damage, but this was not at all the object of the exercise, and it was always a cause for rejoicing when they did not.'[41]

When the above Knight description is taken as being a portion of the *CT*'s ongoing allegorical theme we pay more attention to the thought that Chaucer could here be describing himself as having, through the medium of his art, fought 'for oure feith'within his own personality, and by so doing vanquished 'the three enemys of mankynde, that is to sayn, the flesh, the feend, and the world.' (*Mel* 1421) Elsewhere Chaucer selects the word 'slay' in such a figurative sense: 'And thus: Certes, synful mannes soule is betraysed of the devel by coveitise of temporeel prosperitee, and scorned by deceite whan he cheseth fleshly delices; and yet is it tormented by inpacience of adversitee and bispet by servage and subjeccioun of synne; and atte laste it is slayn finally. / For this disordinanunce of synful man was Jhesu Crist first bitraysed.' (ParsT 276-77)

In the above comment Chaucer appears to be stating that art follows religion in aspiring towards the higher spiritual level of human discernment and goodness. If this was his intention, then the anagram that forms itself out of the word 'Tramyssene'= my-art-sense, could be very significant. The frontage of Paul Piehler's book has the following on such a form of composition:

---

[41]Jones, Terry, *Chaucer's Knight, The Portrait of a Medieval Mercenary*, London, 1980. (pp. 81-82)

'Attempts to demonstrate that imaginative participation in the experience of allegorical vision was in itself a mode of soul healing and psychic integration.'[42] Elsewhere in Chaucer's works we find a call on Appollo: 'God of science and of light,' to guide his 'art poetical' into 'sumwhat agreable' so that 'devyne vertu' may 'entre in my brest anoon!' (*HF Bk.* III, 1091-1109)

Having arrived at this consideration it was pleasing for me to find that Professor Robertson had come to the following conclusion regarding the predominately Christian ideal that could underline a knightly presentation. He explains this with a far greater knowledge and better scholarship than I possess: 'External knighhood is a figure for internal knighthood, and without the internal, the external is vain and empty. And just as there are two parts of a man, corporal and spiritual, so there are two swords proper to defense against the various enemies of man: the material, with which injuries are repelled, and the spiritual, with which those things which injure the mind are repelled. Whence it is said, "Behold, there are two swords." (Luke 22. 38) The knight should gird on the external one to keep temporal peace safe from violence, and the internal one, which is the sword of the Word of God, to restore peace to his own breast ... Alanus goes on to

---

[42] Piehler, Paul, The Visionary Landscape: A Study in Medieval Allegory. Edward Arnold (Publishers) Ltd, London, 1971.

say that the knight should arm himself with the breastplate of faith, gird on the sword of God's word, take up the lance of charity, and put on the helmet of salvation. Thus armed, he confronts the triple enemy: the devil, the world, and the flesh.'[43]

When we have recognized the Knight to be a representative of Chaucer the following description: 'He nevere yet no vileynye ne sayde / In al his lyf unto no maner wight,' (*GP* 70-71) establishes that the criticisms he directs towards the hidden figures within his allegories are those of a person that attempts to correct sinful behaviour by means of the truthfulness of his moral sentences. To establish further this importance we find that the Narrator concludes his *General Prologue* with a precise definition of this word *vileynye*: 'But first I pray yow, of youre curteisye, / That ye n'arette it nat my vileynye, / Thogh that I pleynly speke in this mateere;' (*GP* 725-27) 'Crist spak himself ful brode in hooly writ, / And wel ye woot no vileynye is it. / Eek Plato seith, whoso kan hym rede, / The wordes moote be cosyn to the dede.' (*GP* 739-42)

(King Richard / the Squire)

The Knight is accompanied by the figure of King Richard as the young Squire disposition:

---

[43] Robertson, pp. 174-75.

'With hym ther was his sone, a yong Squire.' (*GP* 79) Such a father / son pairing was then considered the respectful way of denoting a tutor / pupil relationship. Chaucer probably formed such a connection of himself and the young Squire as a means of establishing the Squire's identification, and with this a token of his own intention to counsel the real-life person figured as this pilgrim. The extant paintings of the twenty year old King Richard convey a remarkable similarity of appearance to this Squire presentation: 'With lokkes crulle as they were leyd in presse. / Of twenty yeer of age he was, I gesse.' (*GP* 81-82)

When in France with his warring father, Richard would have been too young to have taken part in serious cavalry raids; because of this it seems to follow that the Squire's identity in such a direct manner as is believed to be found in the Knight's portrayal would not have been Chaucer's intention. A more hidden way of understanding this 'somtyme in chyvachie' (*GP* 85) was therefore required; eventually, I arrived at what I considered could be the most likely explanation of his 'chyvachie / In Flaundres, in Artoys, and Pycardie.' (GP 85-86)

Although very tentatively, for this is surely the most difficult part of the *General Prologue* to explain to myself, and therefore will definitely be so regarding the reader's acceptance of it, I am inclined to consider that this particular Squire description could have been a humourous reference to a time shortly after Richard's birth; perhaps to that period when the five years old young prince had been given a demonstrating 'experience' of accompanying his father, Edward the warring Black Prince, on one of his 'chyvachie' campaigns on the Continent. Apparently these 'chyvachie' raids were not pitched battles, they signified no more than marauding rides that stamped the overlord's formidable presence over a conquered territory. Under Edward's command they represented a policy of disrupting the resources and of alarming the inhabitants of the territories being held.[44] If this was Chaucer's intention with this presentation, then we should pause a little longer over the above mention of 'somtyme in chyvachie.'

Likewise the following description: 'Born hym weel, as of so litel space, / In hope to stonden in his lady grace,' (*GP* 87-8) could also be a teasing linkage of the young prince's birth and to that time shortly following the event. Certainly, the comments: 'Of his stature he was of evene length, / wonderly delyvere, and of greet strengthe,' (*GP* 89-90) may also have been intended as being those complimentary remarks as often accompanies the birth of a newly born baby boy. Elsewhere Chaucer

[44] Coredon, Christoper, *A Dictionary of Medieval Terms & Phrases*, 2004, D.S. Brewer, Cambridge. (pp.70-71)

applies the word 'delivered' to a new birth: 'The letter spak the queene delivered was.' (*MLT* 750)

Unlike the Knight's plainness of clothing: 'He was nat gay. / Of fustian he wered a gypon / Al bismotred wih his habergeon,' this Squire portrayal indicates King Richard's love of flowery dress and courtly accomplishments: 'Embrouded was he, as it were a meede / Al ful of fresshe floures, whyte and reede. / Syngynge he was, or floytynge, al the day; / He was as fresh as is the month of May. / Short was his gowne, with sleves longe and wyde. / Wel koude he sitte on hors and faire ryde. / He koude songes make and wel endite, / Juste and eek daunce, and weel purtreye and write.' (GP 89-96) Nigel Saul presents us with an interesting comment that suggests to me that Chaucer could have pointed out the Squire's identity in greater detail than has been previously assumed: 'Richard's upbringing in his years of boyhood or 'pueritia' would probably have followed the pattern usual among the aristocracy ... By his teens he would also have been given his first taste of music ... it is clear that music regularly formed part of young aristocrats' upbringing. The pupils were taught to harp, pipe and to sing; they may even have been taught rudimentary composition. There are signs that Richard developed some expertise in music.'[45]

---

[45] Saul, p. 14.

The one disturbing detail to be found in this otherwise pleasing presentation of the cultivated young Squire being the description: 'So hoote he lovede that by nyghtertale / He sleep namoore than dooth a nyghtyngale.' (*GP* 97-8) Such destructive 'hot' *cupiditas* love emotions torment Palamon and Arcite in the *Knight's Tale*; and because of this the tale's figure of Emelye entreats Diana her chaste goddess to ensure: 'that al hire hoote love and hir desire, / And al hir bisy torment, and hir fir / Be queynt, or turned in another place.' (*KnT* 2319-21). Elsewhere Chaucer cautions those possessing such hot 'blynde lust, the which that may nat laste,' to turn away from such a sensual form of loving:

> O yonge, fresshe folks, he or she,
> In which that love up groweth with youre age,
> Repeyreth hom fro worldly vanyte,
> And of your herte up casteth the visage
> To thilke God that after his ymage
> Yow made, and thynketh al nys but a faire,
> This world that passeth soone as floures faire.
> And loveth hym the which that right for love
> Upon a crois, oure soules for to beye,
> First starf, and roos, and sit in hevene above;
> For he nyl falsen no wight, dar I seye,
> That wol his herte al holly on hym leye.

And syn he best to love is, and most meke,
What nedeth feynede loves for to seke?
(*Tr.* Bk V. 1835-1848)

(King Richard / the Yeoman)

From here onwards the allegorical arrangment of the General Prologue begins to consolidate into a greater clarity of purpose. When considered together with his close companion the Squire; this Yeoman presentation implies that 'at that tyme' the young King Richard's personality was a combination of the courtly Squire disposition and this outdoor Yeoman. The previous Squire finery of courtly attire being complemented in the Yeoman's equally conspicuous woodland costume: 'A Yeman hadde he and servantz namo / At that tyme, for hym list ride so, / And he was clad in cote and hood of grene. / A sheef of pecok arwes, bright and kene, / Under his belt he bar ful thriftily / (Wel koude he dresse his takel yemanly; / His arwes drouped noght with fetheres lowe), And in his hand he baar a myghty bowe.' (*GP* 101-08)

King Richard's passion for hunting and of his wearing of such expensive outdoor ornamentation have been well documented. Evidently he had also possessed such items as this Yeoman's 'gay daggere' and the 'horn' that hung on a girdle decorated with green tassels of silk: 'An horn he bar, the bawdryk was of grene.' (*GP* 116) Nigel Saul informs us: 'Every summer as king he repaired to the forests of Woodstock, Rockingham or the New Forest, and his love of the chase is attested by his purchase from a London goldsmith in 1386 of a knife to be used in woods and a hunting horn of gold, embellished with green tassels of silk.'[46] Notice here that these items of dagger and horn are said to have been purchased in 1386, the year in which the Squire version of King Richard approximated the above: 'Of twenty yeer of age he was, I gesse.' (*GP* 82) Richard was born at Bordeaux on January 6th 1367.

(Queen Isabel / the Prioress)

The Prioress presents us with an innocent and a seemingly religious representative of Queen Isabel. At seven years of age this French child princess became King Richard's second wife: 'The Prioress has attracted more commentary and controversy than almost any other character to be found in the *General Prologue.*' (*Riverside* p. 803) I believe that such confusion is due to the inability of previous readers to consider these pilgrims as being allegorical representatives of real-life persons. Such an oversight resulting in the required bringing

---

[46] Saul, p. 15.

together of such matters as are declared to be the: 'Engagingly imperfect submergence of the feminine in the ecclesiastical.'[47]

No such problems arise when the Prioress is understood to be a figurative stand-in for Queen Isabel, the seven year old daughter of the French King Charles VI. There are many hints of her connection with France: 'symple and coy,' (*GP* 119) 'The phrase is common in French courtly poetry.' (*Riverside*, p. 803) 'Eglentyne' (Fr. Eglantine; O. Fr. Aiglent) being the French word for the English 'honeysuckle' flower. Another marker being that 'Hire gretteste ooth was but by seint Loy;' (*GP* 120) 'Eloy' being the name of a former goldsmith and keeper of the French royal mint, this oath implies both her membership with the French royal family and, as will be seen later, prepares us to anticipate her desire to possess an abundance of those material advantages that gold acquires a person.

Probably we should also be aware that the Prioress pronounces the saint's name as 'Loy;' this being the clipped and more familiar form of the French Eloy; Saint Eligius to the English. The description: 'Ful weel she soong the service dyvyne, / Entuned in hir nose ful seemly,' (*GP* 122-23) could be another indication of Madame

---

[47] *Riverside*, p. 803.

Eglentyne's close familiarity with spoken French: a language characterised by its nasal intonation. Such an abundance of connections with France close on what appears to be an wry denial that her 'faire / very good' and 'fetisly / elegant' command of the French language is not to be taken as being that of Queen Isabel's native city of Paris: 'And Frenssh she spak ful faire and fetisly, / After the scole of Stratford atte Bowe / For Frenssh of Parys was to hire unknowe.' (*GP* 124-26)

This portrayal also presents powerful hints of the young queen's childhood: 'For, hardily, she was not undergrowe;' (*GP* 156) such a phrase may well have its modern equivalent in the compliment that a particular child is 'tall for its age.' Another such childhood hint could be: 'Of small coral aboute hire arm she bar.' (*GP* 158) Coral was then considered to be a special charm in the protection of children: 'The bells on an infant's coral were a Roman Catholic addition to frighten away evil spirits.'[48] The description of her crying on seeing a trapped, a bleeding or a dead mouse, and also her tearful responses at the misfortunes of her dogs, suggest a child's reaction rather than those of a mature woman charged with the management duty of a priory.

---

[48] Brewer's Dictionary of Phrase and Fable, Cassell Publishers, 1992, (p. 268).

Probably the unbelievable richness of the nourishment she lavishes on her pets: 'Of smale houndes hadde she that she fedde / With rosted flesh, or milk and wastel-breed,' (*GP* 146-47) is intended to be contrasted with the abject poverty suffered by this young queen's subjects: 'The size and terms of the grants (1397) represented a major victory for the king. He had successfully overridden the view of taxation as justified only by the exceptional needs of the realm and had opened the way to the imposition of taxation in time of truce or peace. It was the notoriety of this which Henry IV exploited in 1399 when he accused Richard of taxing his people heavily "while the kingdom was not burdened with the expense of war." Such an extension of the grounds of public taxation to meet the peacetime costs of government was seen as a threat to the property and liberty of the subject.'[49]

Being the premier metal, gold was a symbol of royalty, and the closing description implies a further hint of her identity: 'And theron heng a brooch of gold ful sheene, / On which ther was first write a crowned A, / And after *Amor vincit omnia.*' (*GP* 160-62) Notice here that the Prioress's brooch and its golden crown presents us with telling indicators of her sovereignty; the letter 'A' on her brooch, and it being a 'crowned A,' signifying the

---

[49] Saul, pp. 260-61.

Prioress' foremost female position within her society. The *'Amor vincit omnia* / love conquers all' inscription on her brooch will later be understood to represent *cupiditas* / sensual love rather than the desirable *caritas* / charitable form.

(Queen Isabel / the Second Nun)

Her closeness to the Prioress and the lack of any other detailed description: 'Another nonne with hire hadde she, / That was hir chapeleyne;' (*GP* 163-64) also the similarities of their prologues and tales, such linkages as these suggest the Second Nun to be another religious representative of Queen Isabel. Tyrwhitt summarised this Second Nun's presentation with the following comment: 'The single circumstance of description is false; for no Nonne could be a Chaplain. The chief duty of a Chaplain was to say Mass, and to hear Confession, neither of which offices could regularly be performed by a Nonne or by any woman'.[50]

---

[50] Tyrwhitt, Thomas, *The Poetical Works of Geoffrey Chaucer*, London, (1883), p. lii. See also his note: 'It appears that some Abbesses did at one time attempt to hear the Confessions of their Nuns, and to exercise some other smaller parts of the clerical functions; but this practice, I apprehend, was soon stopped by Gregory IX'. Gregory IX was Pope in an earlier period of the Church's history, from March 19th. 1227 to August 22, 1241.

(King Richard / the Monk)

The first line of this introduction implies the Monk's hidden sovereignty: 'A monk ther was, a fair for the maistrie.' (*GP* 165) Tyrwhitt's gloss on the line suggests a greater relevance than is now taken: 'As to the phrase for the maistrie, I take it to be derived from the French *pour la maistrie*, which I find, in an old book of Physick, applied to such medicines as we usually call *Sovereign*, excellent above all others.'[51] King Richard's anointment at his coronation also appears to be hinted: 'His heed was baled, that shoon as any glas, / And eek his face, as he hadde been enoynt.' (*GP* 198-99)

This Monk is said to belong to 'the reule of Seint Maure or of Seint Beneit;' (*GP* 173) this Seint Maure description implies a probable connection with the Prioress from her Benedictine nunnery of Stratford atte Bowe. Although St. Benedict founded the first monastery of this order at Monte Cassino, between Naples and Rome, it was the above Seint Maure that introduced the Benedictine rule into France. Apparently as long as the Benedictines remained poor they were a blessing to the countries in which they lived, spending as they did several hours a day in gardening and in agriculture; besides this they held schools outside the walls of their

---

[51] ibid. p. 174.

convents. Science and literature are also indebted to them for having copied many the classical authors and preserved such knowledge as existed in their age. But when at length their merits had drawn much wealth to their order, luxury and indolence sapped their virtues and diminished their influence for good.

Although the Narrator appears to be declaring himself doubtful to which of these very different ways of communal existence this Monk belongs, the descriptions he presents throughout the presentation emphasise his preference: 'A Monk ther was, a fair for the maistrie / An outridere, that lovede venerie.... / A fat swan loved he best of any roost. / His palfrey was as broun as is a berye.' (*GP* 165-207) The line: 'Grehoundes he hadde as swift as fowel in flight,' (*GP* 190) complement the 'smale houndes' kept by the Prioress. 'And for to festne his hood under his chyn / He hadde of gold ywroght a ful curious pyn; / A love-knotte in the gretter end ther was,' (*GP* 195-97) recalls her gold brooch with its 'love conquers all' motto. The outrageous lackness displayed in this portrayal appears intended to be such as would immediately have alerted and therby encouraged Chaucer's contemporaries to question and identify this unlikely representative of the Christian religion.

Probably the lines: 'He was nat pale as a forpyned goost, / A fat swan loved he best of any roost;' (*GP* 206) implies King Richard's revengeful execution / 'roasting' of Thomas of Woodstock / Duke of Gloucester: the leader of the 1386-88 appellants By means of identification of their emblematic badges the contemporary poet of *Richard the Redeless* indicates those Richard believed to be his enemies; Thomas of Gloucester being plainly figured as the swan of the following line: 'Ne to stryue with swan though it sholle were.'[52]

(King Richard / the Friar)

Unfavourable behavioural changes is seen to have taken place between the young Squire figure of King Richard and this later Friar version of what was earlier described to be the 'hot' young Squire disposition. The Squire presentation: 'Curteis he was, lowely, and servysable,' (*GP* 99) has now been given a subtle but nevertheless a highly significant change of phrase: 'Curteis he was and lowely of servyse.' (*GP* 250) The previous Squire disposition of civility, of humbleness and willingness to serve, having here been replaced by the 'lowly / poor quality' of this Friar's service. The line: 'Wel koude he synge and playen on a rote,' (*GP* 236) recalls the Squire's musical talents: 'Syngynge he was, or

---

[52]Barr. Helen,, Passus II, (p. 116). 1993.

floytynge, al the day;' (*GP* 91) 'therto he strong was as a champioun,' (*GP* 239) complements the earlier Squire description of his 'greet strengthe.' (*GP* 84) King Richard's foremost position within the hierarchy of the feudal government also appears to be implied in the following: 'Unto his ordre he was a noble post.' (*GP* 214)

The description: 'He hadde maad ful many a marriage / Of yonge women at his owene cost,' (*GP* 212-13) implies King Richard's granting of marriage dowries in order to be unburdened of redundant mistresses. It is recorded that as early as December 1384: 'He gave no less than £200 to one of his esquires, John Rose, to assist him with his marriage.'[53] The historical records indicate that following Queen Anne's death, and certainly from 1396 onwards, the females at the royal court profited greatly from his extravagances: 'Contemporaries commented on the number of ladies who thronged his court. It is noticeable that from 1396 the courtier ladies benefited more than before from his partronage. A particular favourite appears to have been Blanche, Lady Poynings. In 1397 Richard presented her with a precious ring, and in the following year he granted her £40 "of his gift." It is hard to know what degree of affection lay behind Richard's favour to Lady Poynings and her

---

[53] Saul, p. 458.

like.'[54] When we come to understand that this Friar is a lustful and extravagant portrayal of King Richard; we probably gain a better understanding of the above described relationship concerning the king and 'Blanche, Lady Poynings.'

The Friar's real-life identity also appears to be implied in the following lines: 'Ful sweetly herde he confessioun, / And plesaunt was his absolucioun.' (*GP* 221-22) 'Plesaunt' and 'absolucioun' being terms that hint those final years of King Richard's tyranny. The historical reality here being that on the pretext they had previously supported his political opponents he had compelled many of his subjects to obtain what became known as his 'absolution' pardons; also blank charters that at any time he desired allowed him to claim arbitrarily selected sums of money from his subjects: these were termed '*Le Plesaunce.*'

Such behaviour against the interests of his subjects became a significant condemnation when it eventually came to assessing the necessity of Richard's dethronement. His extravagance and his constant need of money in the final years of the reign ensured that 'he was the beste beggere in his hous; / (And yaf a certeyn ferme for the graunt; (251-252a) / Noon of his bretheren cam ther in his haunt; 252b) / For thogh a wydwe hadde noght a

---

[54]Ibid. p.454.

sho, / So plesaunt was his '*In principio,*' / Yet wolde he have a ferthyng, er he wente.' (*GP* 252-255) The historical reality is that: 'No English records show that friars paid a fee (ferme) for rights, exclusive or otherwise, to operate within a district, or limitation.'(*Riverside,* p. 808)

In those final years of his reign Richard's subjects greatly feared his anger: 'And rage he koude, as it were right a whelp.' (*GP* 257) Such displays of his uncontrollably violent behaviour are encountered in the historical records: 'There is no evidence of madness in the king, just an ever-inceasing tendncy to rule his subjects throught the medium of terror. In explaining their actions in 1397-8, the lords who were later arraigned for treason all pleaded that they carried out his commands because they had been frightened of the king. It was a genuine excuse; anyone in their position would have been scared.'[55] We also find the following: 'The king's nature, since Richard was ten had been known ... its capriciousness, its murderous rages.'[56]

The description: 'In love-dayes (days for settling disputes out of court) ther koude he muchel help,' (*GP* 258) immediately directs our attention to

---

[55] Mortimer, Ian, The Fears of Henry IV, The Life of England's Self-Made King, Jonathan Cape. London, 2007. (p.. 136)
[56] Bruce, Marie Louise, The Usurper King: Henry of Bolingbroke 1366-99, The Rubicon Press, n.d., (p. 176).

Richard's advantageous political intervention in the trial by combat that he had arranged to take place between Henry Bolingbroke and Thomas Mowbray in 1398. His intrusion in that event providing him with the excuse to banish overseas the remaining younger two of the former appellants to his earlier misrule: 'Sir John Bushy came forward to announce the king's decision: Hereford was to be banished from the realm for ten years, and Norfolk for life. A huge outcry acompanied the announcement of Hereford's sentence, for the duke was the popular favourite.'[57]

(King Richard / the Nun's Priest)

Being that the term 'priest' could be applied to any ordained person who performed the sacred rites and intervened between the worshipper and God, there seems no valid reason why the Monk, Friar and the Nun's Priest, should not be taken as being the three priests / 'and preestes thre,' (*GP* 165) said to accompany the Prioress on the pilgrimage. Our acceptance of this group bringing the total number of pilgrims to the 'nyne and twenty' that are described to have gathered at the Tabard.

---

[57] Saul, p. 401.

Notice the conspicuous eyes described to be possessed by each of these three priests: the Monk has 'eyen stepe, and rollynge in his heed, / That stemed as a forneys of a leed;' (*GP* 201-02) the Friar's 'eyen twinkled in his heed aright / As doon the sterres in the frosty nyght,' (*GP* 267-68) and the Nun's Priest 'loketh as a sperhauk with his yen.' (*NPT* 3457) Being another prominent version of King Richard, it's not surprisingly that the Host is also described to have 'eyen stepe.'(*GP* 753) Although I have not as yet come across any historical description that depicts King Richard possessing such distinctive eyes, I think it more than likely that somewhere or other in the contemporary records evidence of such as this oft-repeated feature may be waiting to be discovered.

(King Richard / the Merchant)

The closing line of the Friar presentation: 'This worthy lymytour was cleped Huberd,' (*GP* 269) suggests this fork-bearded Merchant to be another representative of King Richard. When the king's body was exhumed for inspection in 1871 his remains were found to contain traces of a 'hued' and a double pointed (forked) beard, such as that possessed by the Merchant. That the Merchant 'wolde the see were kept for any thyng / Bitwixe Middelburgh and Orewelle,' (*GP* 276-77) indicates

King Richard's concern for the protection of the route that conveyed his ownership of the highly profitable Wool Staple; probably this form of royal commerce with the weavers of Flanders is also the reason for his wearing a 'Flaundryssh bever hat.' (*GP* 271)

The Merchant presentation indicates the swaggering king's reckless attitude towards his financial debt: 'Wel koude he in eschaunge sheeldes selle. / This worthy man ful wel his wit bisette: / Ther wiste no wight that he was in dette, / So estatly was he of his governaunce / With his bargynes and with his chevyssaunce.' (*GP* 278 - 282) There must have been many times when the extravagant sovereign's inability to remain within his spending limits would have become very obvious to his subjects: 'After 1395 the deficits returned, and by 1398 the king was spending over £11,000 a year more than he received.'[58] Of course, not only was this pilgrim's name known to the Narrator: 'But, sooth to seyn, I noot how men hym calle,' (*GP* 284) it would also have been very obvious to all those others that were capable of understanding these ongoing allegories.

---

[58] Saul, p. 259.

(Chaucer / the Clerk)

A respectful tone identical to that found in the Knight's presentation returns in this portrayal of Chaucer as the Clerk that had 'longe ygo' studied at Oxford. This pilgrim is portrayed to be worthy of the highest esteem: 'Of studie took he moost cure and moost heede. / Noght o word spak he moore than was neede, / And that was seyd in form and reverence, / And short and quyk and ful of hy sentence.' (*GP* 303-06) Hoccleve's description of Chaucer as being 'Aristotle in our tonge' being plainly evidenced in this presentation of the Clerk: 'For hym was levere have at his beddes heed / Twenty bookes, clad in blak or reed, / Of Aristotle and his philosophie / Than robes riche, or fithele, or gay sautrie.' (*GP* 293-96).

The previous description of the arrogant Merchant: 'Sowynge alwey th'encrees of his wynnyng;' (*GP* 275) is contrasted here in this Clerk description: 'Sowynge in moral vertu was his speche, / And gladly wolde he lerne and gladly teche.' (*GP* 307-308) The Clerk is one of those pilgrims that, obviously incorrectly in my opinion, others have believed it to be worth attempting to identify him outside such an allegorical dimension: 'The Clerk has often been identified with well-known schoolmen of Chaucer's time. Ussery (TSE 18, 1970, 1-15) reviews thirty-six prominent Oxford logicians of the fourteenth century. Most possible models were associated with Merton College.'[59]

(King Richard / the Man of Law)

The Merchant's 'motley' dress has now been given its multicoloured equivalent in the Man of Law's 'medley' coat: 'He rood but hoomly in a medlee cote.' (*GP* 328) This presentation figures King Richard's constant examination of the Law for those royal advantages that allowed him to confiscate the properties of his subjects. The following description: 'A Sergeant of the Lawe, war and wys, / That often hadde been at the Parvys, / Ther was also, ful riche of excellence. / He semed swich, his wordes weren so wise;' (*GP* 309-10) immediately draws our attention to the above 'semed;'that is, the Narrator is not actually affirming the Man of the Law to be 'war and wys,' rather than this he is informing us that his speech 'seems' to give that impression.

Once we become aware of this pilgrims identity we are not surprised to find that the above 'Parvys' signified a church porch location were matters of contestable legalities within the Law were often disputed. Instituted in the early feudalism of William the Conqueror, the primary

---

[59] *Riverside*, p. 810.

purpose of the 'parvys' was to recover debts of property and any other sums of money that could be considered owing to the Crown: 'There was one at St. Paul's Cathedral in London and it was there in the 14c that lawyers met for talk, disputation and consultation.'[60]

The tyrannical Richard's attempts to return the country's laws back to those earlier 'fee simple' days are certainly implied in the following description: 'So greet a purchasour was nowher noon: / Al was fee simple to hym in effect; / His purchasing might nat been infect.' (*GP* 318-20) That is, this Man of Law disposition attempts to re-establish the earlier period of the Norman Conquest; a time when the sovereign held an unassailable right of property: 'In termes hade he caas and doomes alle / That from the tyme of kyng William were falle. / Therto he koude endite and make a thyng, / Ther koude no wight pynche at his writing.' (*GP* 323-26)

The abdication charges of 1399 contained numerous accusations of Richard's disregard for what had become accepted as the traditionally established rights of his subjects: 'Item, being unwilling to protect and preserve the just laws and customs of he realm ... Frequently, from time to time, when the laws were declared and set forth to

---

[60]Coredon, Christopher, p. 211.

him by the Justices and others of his Council, and he should have done justice to those who sought it according to those laws - he said expressly, with harsh and insolent looks, that his laws were in his mouth, and some-times within his breast; and that he alone could change or establish the laws of his realm. Deceived by which opinion, he would not allow justice to be done to many of his lieges, but compelled numbers of persons to desist from suing common right by threats and fear.'[61]

(King Richard / the Franklin)

The Franklin companion of the Man of Law: 'A Frankeleyn was in his compaignye,' (*GP* 331) implies a future version of King Richard: 'Whit was his berd as is the dayesye.' (*GP* 332) His later interruption of the *Squire's Tale* presents us with an interesting trio: the former eloquent Squire: '"In feith, Squier, thow hast thee wel yquit / And gentilly. I preise wel thy wit," / Quod the Frankeleyn "considerynge thy yowthe, / So feelingly thou spekest, sire, I allow the! / As to my doom, ther is noon that is heere / Of eloquence that shal be thy peere, / If that thou lyve; God yeve thee good chaunce, / And in vertu sende thee continuaunce, / For of thy speche I have greet

---

[61] Hughes, Dorothy, p. 291.

deyntee;'" (*SqT* 673-681) this future dispirited Franklin disposition implies that the Squire did not retain such virtuous promise as that to be found in his earlier speech: 'I have a sone, and by the Trinitee, / I hadde levere than twenty pound worth lond, / Though it right now were fallen in myn hond, / He were a man of swich discrecioun / As that ye been! Fy on possessioun, / But if a man be vertuous withal! / I have my sone snybbed, and yet shal, / For he to vertu listeth nat entende; / But for to pleye at dees, and to despende / And lese al that he hath is his usage. / And he hath levere talken with a page / Than to commune with any gentil wight / Where he myghte lerne gentillesse aright.' (*SqT* 682-694) Finally, we have the Host disposition affirming King Richard's present lack of virtuous speech towards others: '"Straw for your gentillesse!" quod oure Hoost.' (*SqT* 695).

This figure of the Franklin presents a warning to those who assume that a life of sensuality is a means of achieving lasting happiness: 'To liven in delit was evere his wone, / For he was Epicurus owene sone, / That heeld opinioun that pleyn delit / Was verray felicitee parfit.' (*GP* 335-338) The contrary of the belief expressed in the above comment is found in the *Prosa* 7 passage from Chaucer's *Boece*: 'But what schal I seye of delyces of body, of whiche delices the desirynges ben ful of anguyssch, and the fulfillynges of hem ben ful of penance? How grete seknesses and how grete sorwes unsuffrable, ryght as a maner fruyt of wykkidnesse, ben thilke delices wont to bryngen to the bodyes of folk that usen hem ... And the gladnesse of wyf and children were an honest thyng, but it hath ben seyd that it is overmochel ayens kynde that children han ben fownden tormentours to here fadris, I not how manye; of whiche children how bytynge is every condicioun, it nedeth nat to tellen it the that hast er this tyme assayed it, and art yit now angwyssh.' (Riverside, p. 427)

The gastronomic excesses within the Franklin's household: 'It snewed in his hous of mete and drynke; / Of alle deyntees that men koude thynke,' (*GP* 345-46) portrays the historical reality of King Richard's court: '*The Forme of Cury,* the first English cookery book, was compiled about 1390 by the royal court's master cook. A renowned 'gourmet, King Richard has been described as "the best and ryallest vyander of alle christen kynges." The book consists of 196 recipes ... Entire joints of meat were never served, fish and fowl being usually hacked and cut into pieces or gobbets ... Deer's livers and hares' flesh often formed the basis of enormous pates, while another recipe was of gele (jelly) of fish consisting of eel and turbot. Olive oil rather than butter formed the basis of cooking and 'lumbard mustard' from Italy was very popular.

Saffron if often mentioned, imported from Egypt, Cilicia or other parts of the Levant and much used, and also for colouring and garnishing,'[62]

Information of the festive splendour at the royal court, details of which can only be touched upon here, and that solely in order to show the correctness of the *General Prologue's* description of this Franklin disposition comes in the Narrator's: 'Seint Julian, he was in his contree.' (*GP* 340) 'The Monk of Westminster, probably the best-informed writer of the reign, provides a remarkable description of the king's reception of the exiled king, Leo of Armenia in 1385: Leo "was welcomed by the king," he says, "and was enriched by a quantity of truly splendid gifts and presents ... An attractive account is also given by the same writer of the Duke of Guelder's reception in London in 1390. The duke, he says, was personally greeted by the king, "who feasted him sumptuously and plied him with lavish enterainments, including dancing and a pleasing variety of instrumental music and paid him every flattering attention."'[63]

(King Richard / the Guildsmen)

The *General Prologue's* well ordered presentation of pilgrims has this group of the five

---

[62] Bevan, Bryan, King Richard II, (1990), Rubicon Press, pp.84-85.
[63] Saul, pp. 336-37)

Guildsmen set between two groups of twelve others: Knight, Squire, Yeoman, Prioress, Second Nun, the three Priests: Monk / Friar / Nun's Priest; Merchant, Clerk, Man of Law, Franklin, **Guildsmen**, Cook, Shipman, Doctor, Wife of Bath, Parson, Plowman, Miller, Manciple, Reeve, Somonour, Pardoner, and Chaucer the Narrator.

Unless Chaucer intended us to question the unusual singleness of this group: 'An Haberdasshere and a Carpenter, / A Webbe, a Dyere, and a Tapycer - / And they were clothed alle in o lyveree;' (*GP* 361-63) it's difficult to understand why he had inserted a carpenter into the company of four members of the cloth workers guild. I believe that the non-allegorical explanations now presented as valid reasons are incorrect: 'Their great *fraternitee* is probably not one of the craft guilds, which were usually composed of practitioners of a single trade ... The Carpenter would be an unlikely member of the Drapers. Instead, they are probably members of one of the parish guilds, fraternal and charitable organizations ... Garbaty makes a strong case for the guild of St. Botolph's in Aldersgate, but such identifications can be only speculative.'[64]

Skeat noted that this group contravened the sumptuary law of 1363. Such a description as 'Hir

---

[64] *Riverside*, p. 813.

knyves was chaped noght with bras / But al with silver,' I consider to be a prompting of our need to question their identities; that is we once again confront such doubtful detail as when the earlier Yeoman was described to be wearing 'A Cristopher on his brest of silver sheene.'(*GP* 115) The line: 'For catel hadde they ynogh and rente,' (*GP* 373) presents the interpretive problem of why, if considered outside such an allegorical framework, that these five possessors of great wealth are also described as being members of the craft industries. The reference to their wives: 'It is ful fair to been ycleped "madame," And goon to vigilies al before, / And have a mantel roialliche ybore,' (*GP* 378) connects them with 'Madame' Eglentyne the Prioress; and also with the Wife of Bath's fondness of 'visitaciouns / To vigilies and to processiouns.' However slightly hinted, their royal status may also be implied in the above 'mantel roialliche ybore' decription.

(King Richard / the Cook)

This Cook tends to be generally considered as 'a concoction of culinary superlatives, telling us nothing of his personality, except what is suggested by his knowledge of London ale.' I believe that when it's read as an allegorical presentation this figure depicts both King Richard's gluttony and, far more serious than this, the murderous nature of his tyranny.

The Cook is named as Roger, Hogge of Ware. The name 'Roger' points us to the French word *rogue* / cheat, / Eng. rogue; -ry; 'hogge' indicates a piggish presence, and 'ware' implies the need for others to 'beware' of his behaviour. Probably the word 'ware' conveys such as 'let hym be war! His nekke lith to wedde.' (*KnT* 1218) This 'Hogge' is a 'stynkyng swyn,' (*MancT* 40) and 'Perkyn' the commonest of pig names is given to his tale's presentation of the eventually dismissed apprentice. I find it interesting that Chaucer possessed such knowledge as is shown in his awareness of a pig's ecstatic delight on having its back scratched; surely this is what best explains the later description of the Cook's pleasurable response to the *Reeve's Tale*: 'For joye him thought he clawed him on the bak.' (*CkT Pro* 4326)

This Cook recalls the *Odyssey* episode when Circe transforms the gluttonous into swine: 'Soon in the luscious feast themselves they lost, / And drank oblivion of their native coast. / Instant her circling wand the goddess waves, / To hogs transforms them, and the sty receives.'[65] Chaucer was certainly aware of the Circe figure, and also of the gluttonous associations being figured in the *Odyssey*: 'Ther

---

[65] The Odyssey of Homer, trans. Alexander Pope, London.(n.d), (p. 137).

saugh I the, quene Medea / And Circes eke.' (*HF* 1271-72) Perhaps the Cook's scabbed ulcer: 'But greet harm was it, as it thought me, / That on his shyne a mormal hadde he,' (*GP* 385-86) is also taken from classical literature. Diogenes Laertius informs us that the Greek poet Alcaeus referred to the tyrant of his day as 'chap-foot' because of the cracks in his feet.'[66] Chaucer was certainly aware of the works of Diogenes, and also of its portraying the greed that motivated tyrants into their foreign ventures:

> Thise tyraunts putte hem gladly nat in pres
> No wildnesse ne no bushes for to winne,
> Ther poverte is, as seith Diogenes,
> Ther as vitaile is ek so skars and thinne
> That noght but mast or apples is therinne;
> But, ther as bagges ben a fat vitaile,
> Ther wol they gon, and spare for no sinne
> With al hir ost the cite for to assayle.[67]

We are informed this Cook: 'Koude rooste, and seethe, and broille, and frye, / Maken mortreux, and wel bake a pye.' (*GP* 383-84) Probably these lines allude to King Richard's 'hot' revenge towards those that earlier in the reign had opposed his misrule. It seems to me that *mortreux* is

---

[66]Lives of the Philosophers, Diogenes Laertius, (200-250 A.D.), p. 429.
[67]Riverside, pp. 650-51, *The Former Age.*

intended here to be taken as the plural of *mort* / death; probably this word alludes to the murders of such as the Duke of Gloucester and the Earl of Arundel. 'Wel bake a pye,' recalling his exiling of Thomas Arundel, Archbishop of Canterbury; he being the last of the three leading former appellants. The archbishop was forced to forfeit his properties; due to their black and white vestments bishops were then wittily referred to as magpies / pyes.[68]

The following description is interesting: 'A Cook they hadde with hem for the nones / To boille the chiknes with the marybones, / And poudre-marchant tart and galyngale.' (*GP* 379-81) The word 'nones' is noted elsewhere as signifying 'for the occasion;' this later appears especially significant when we later come to understand that the January disposition in the *Merchant's Tale* requires the assistance of such 'hot' spices before entering the marriage bed with his young wife: 'Spices hoote t'encreessen his corage.' (*MerT* 1808).

(King Richard / the Shipman)

'A shipman was ther, wonynge fer by weste; / For aught I woot, he was of Dertemouthe. / He rood upon a rouncy, as he kouthe.' (*GP* 388-390)

---

[68] Brewer, p, 692.

The first line of this presentation could be punning that this Shipman is 'wonynge' / dwelling in a 'fer' / fair and 'weste' / wasteful manner. Elsewhere we find the description 'wastynge of richesses.' (*Mel* 1392) 'Rouncy' being a term that was then applied to an agricultural horse; the above 'as he kouthe,' implying King Richard's minimal ability to 'ride' the agricultural producers of his wasteful life-style.

I also find the following interesting: 'Of nyce conscience took he no keep, / If that he faught and hadde the hyer hond, / By water he sente hem hoom to every lond.' (*GP* 398-400) Rather than the presently accepted explanation that the Shipman threw his captives overboard, I read this to be a pointer to King Richard's habit of banishing to a new home overseas those he considered to have previously been his political opponents. Such as the above mentioned Archbishop Arundel, and later in the reign Henry Bolingbroke and Thomas Mowbray; when he 'hadde the hyer hond ... by water' they were shipped out of the realm.

The closing final line of this presentation also appears significant: 'His barge ycleped was the Maudelayne.' (*GP* 410) Probably this specific naming of his ship indicates the surname 'Maudelayne;' that of the one recorded to have been entrusted to 'ship' the murdered Duke of

Gloucester's body home from Calais.[69] In 1400 Richard Maudelayne was hanged for the many traitorous crimes he had committed in the former king's service.

(King Richard / the Physician)

This Physician pilgrim is described to be keyed to those times when planetary influences were considered to be the most advantageous for the 'physic' he dispensed to those that are here figured to be 'sick;' King Richard is often reported to have been a keen student of astrology. The line that this Physician 'kepte his pacient a ful greet deel' before dispensing his treatment denotes that lengthy period from the earlier years of his reign to 1397; until that later time when the opportunistic Richard eventually made his move and succeeded in his destruction of the above mentioned members of the former Lord Appellants: 'Anon he yaf the sike man his boote.' (*GP* 424)

In this presentation we also find a hinting of those that to their own profit had assisted the king in his wrongdoings: 'Ful redy hadde he his apothecaries / To sende hym drogges and his letuaries, / For ech of hem made oother for to wynne - / Hir frendshipe nas nat newe to bigynne.'

---

[69] DNB., *Thomas of Woodstock*,(p. 157), Vol. 56, 1898.

(*GP* 425-28) The final lines of the portrayal: 'And yet he was but esy of dispence; / He kepte that he wan in pestilence. / For gold in phisik is a cordial, / Therefore he lovede gold in special,' (*GP* 411-44) implying the financial gains that the royal party amassed when such 'pestilence' brought about the 'ruyne of the hye halles.' (*KnT* 2463)

(Queen Isabel / the Wife of Bath)

The Wife of Bath figure implies a future 'worldly' presentation of the coy Prioress and Second Nun; she is therefore a direct contradiction to the young queen's earlier presentation.

The Narrator's comment on her lack of hearing is humourous: 'She was somdel deaf, and that was scathe.' (*GP* 446) When the work is read in its entirely it's difficult not to believe that the repeated mention of her deafness allude to a domestic assault that took place within the royal household. An otherwise unmentioned incident in which the sometimes uncontrollably violent Richard had slapped his infant wife so hard that it had caused her to suffer a degree of deafness: 'By God, he smoot me ones on the lyst, / For that I rente out of his book a leef, / That of the strook myn ere wax al deef.' (*Pro WBP* 634-36)

Her later comments on the incident in the prologue of her tale adding to the probability of its genuineness: 'Now wol I seye yow sooth, by Seint Thomas, / Why that I rente out of his book a leef, / For which he smoot me so that I was deef;' (*Pro WBP* 666-68) 'But now to purpos, why I tolde thee / That I was beten for a book, pardee!' (*Pro WBP* 711-12) She even presents us with a vivid description of the event: 'He up stirte as dooth a wood leoun, / And with his fest he smoot me on the heed / That in the floor I lay as I were deed;' (*Pro WBP* 794-96) and she adds a vivid description of her own equally violent response: 'I with my fest so took hym on the cheke / That in oure fyr he fil backward adoun.' (*Pro WBP* 792-93)

It's impossible to know for sure whether or not such an incident took place; however, considered together with Harry Bailly's account of his wife being 'byg in armes,' (*Pro MkT* 1921) this description of the Wife of Bath's physical response when angered may provide us with another undiscovered level of Chaucer's humour. Once again I turn to J. Leslie Hotson for what may be the soundest guidance on such descriptions: 'Chaucer's mood complicates his meaning; and his most intricate mood is humour. The greatest rub in the path of understanding it is *partial appreciation.* Our satisfaction at having seen something, one or two points, perhaps, quite prevents us from seeing more. In exploring Chaucer's humour we are sailing on perilous seas; yet it is true that we are in more danger of not seeing his whole meaning than we are of misrepresent what we see. We lose more than we disort.'[70]

Let us now consider further this question of Chaucer's allegorical skills. Whereas critics read the following lines as simply informing us that the Wife of Bath's weaving skills excels that of the Flemish weavers: 'Of clooth-makyng she hadde swich an haunt / She passed hem of Ypres and of Gaunt;' (*GP* 445-46) when these same lines are figuratively considered it appears far more likely Chaucer is implying here that Queen Isabel's purchasing of clothing outstrips the production capacity of the Flemish weavers that were then resident in the city of Bath; then the centre of the English weaving industry. Because they mark the Wife of Bath's partiality for that locality in which cloth was being mass produced, the above words 'Bath' and 'haunt' could therefore be highly significant. Chaucer elsewhere links the word 'haunt' with a particular locality, such an example being when the Parson condemns 'thilke harlots that haunten bordels of thise fool women.' (*ParsT* 885) In the Parson's summary that 'good man of religioun' censures the ruinous social consequences brought about by those who extravagantly overspend on clothes: 'As to the first synne, that is a

---

[70] Hotson, p. 762.

superfluitee of clothynge, which that maketh it so deere, to harm of the peple.' (*ParsT* 416)

The Wife's 'gat-tothed' description has generated a great deal of perplexity. Tyrwhitt treated it with his customary honesty: '(Gat-tothed) whether we read thus, with the generality of the MSS ... or Gap-tothed ... I confess myself equally unable to explain what is meant by this circumstance of description.'[71] Critics now tend towards 'gap-tothed,' and add that 'In medieval physiognomy such teeth indicated an envious, irreverent, luxurious, bold, faithless and suspicious nature.' (*Riverside*, pp. 818-19) I read it that this word 'gat' signifies Alison of Bath's ability to 'gat / get' a superfluousness of life's material goods; this being a 'getting' that she links with the sexual gratification of her various husbands: 'But sith I hadde hem hoolly in myn hond, / And sith they hadde me yeven al hir lond, / What sholde I taken keep hem for to plese, / But it were for my profit and myn ese?' (*WBT* 211-214) She follows this comment with a candid and significant self-analysis: 'But yet I hadde alwey a coltes tooth. / Gat-tothed I was, and that became me weel; / I hadde the prente of seinte Venus seel. / As help me God, I was a lusty oon, / And faire, and riche, and yong and wel bigon.' (*WBT* 602–606) The term

---

[71] Tyrwhitt, (p. 177), note 470.

'colt's tooth' indicated a 'superfluous' tooth found in the mouths of young horses.

(Chaucer / the Parson)

The Parson is 'a lerned man a clerk;' (*GP* 480) he presents a practical version of the studious Clerk of Oxford. Whereas the earlier Clerk aspect of Chaucer was described in terms of 'gladly wolde he lerne and gladly teche;' (*GP* 308) the Parson personifies a commitment to moral guidance through the good instances of his personal behaviour: 'This noble ensample to his sheep he yaf, / That first he wroghte, and afterward he taughte.' (*GP* 496-97)

We eventually become aware that not even the threats of those of 'high estate' are able to intimidate the Parson: 'To drawen folk to hevene by fairnesse, / By good ensample, this was his bisynesse. / But it were any persone obstinate, / What so he were, of heigh or lough estat, / Hym wolde he snybben sharply for the nonys.' (*GP* 519-23) In this presentation Chaucer appears to be inferring his own attempts, initially described to have been carried out through 'fairness,' to persuade King Richard into 'Christes lore and his apostles twelve.' (*GP* 527) It appears however that those efforts had failed and resulted in high powered retaliation against his person: 'Benygne he was, and wonder diligent, / And in adversitee ful pacient, / And swich he was ypreved ofte sithes.' (*GP* 483-85)

Possibly such lines as the above shed light on the actions of Trespass and Contempt (1379) filed against Chaucer in the Rolls of Attorneys 3 Ric. II: 'Trespass consisted of a wide variety of actionable wrongs against the person or property of another ... Actions of contempt lay when there had been contempt of the king's prerogative either by disobeying a writ, summons, or letter, or disobeying an act of parliament.'[72] In the following year a scribbled 'note' recording the Deed of Release against Chaucer for the alleged rape of a Cecily Chaumpaigne is dated on May 4th. That a person of Chaucer's pronounced charitable love towards others could be guilty of such a contemptible offence as rape is hardly worth consideration by those of us that are able to discern his increasingly and long time anguish over the deterioration that he was observing in the behaviour of his sovereign lord.

The best study on this matter of the above mentioned 'note' is that presented by Christopher Cannon. This is not the place for me to delve too deeply into such a detailed investigation as he has clearly demonstrated. Cannon's research involves a

---

[72] Crow and Olson, (pp. 340-42).

knowledge that is far superior to all those others I have come across on this incident, and I would highly recommend it to all those sufficiently interested in this 'partly recorded' incident. The presentation of the lack of 'evidence' to be found regarding this supposed 'rape' strengthens my conviction of its falseness.

The following passages are taken from Cannon's excellent essay: 'On May 4, 1380, Cecily Chaumpaigne brought a deed of release into the Chancery of Richard II and had it enrolled on the close rolls (i.e., recopied by a clerk on the back of those sheets of parchment used to record the "closed" or sealed letters sent by the king.) In this note she is said to have released Chaucer from "all manner of actions such as they relate to my rape or any other thing or cause" ... The deed had been witnessed three days earlier (on May 1, 1380) by several prominent members of the court of Richard II ... The language of this Chaumpaigne release would require comment, however, even if it did not concern a poet as famous as Geoffrey Chaucer simply by virtue of its use of the phrase "*de raptu meo*," which cannot be found in any other document in these rolls ... This memorandum purports to record the language of the Chaumpaigne releases, but its language serves to remind us that the original document is now in fact lost to us ... "*de raptu meo*," as I have also said, is a singular and unusual phrase in the context of contemporary close rolls records ... and it is important to establish the shape of this extended chronology for it bars directly on the differences that exist between the language of the release as it appears in the close rolls and that language as it appears in the memorandum (p.12) ...

The important difference between the two versions of the release language, however, is the absence of the phrase *"de raptu meo"* from the language of the memorandum. Instead of recording a release for "All manner of actions relating to *my rape* or any other thing or cause" ... as the close roll record does, the memorandum shows Cecily Chaumpaigne releasing Chaucer from "All manner of actions both concerning felonies, trespasses, accounts, debts and any other actions whatsoever." The mechanism for this change is far from clear, for without the release itself we cannot be at all sure which of these two reading accurately represents its language (if either one does.) ... Why any one would want to eliminate the phrase *"de raptu meo"* from the memorandum if two other documents containing that language were in existence (that is, the original release and the close rolls record) is harder to explain.'[73]

---

[73] Cannon, Chrisopher, *Raptus in the Chaumpaigne Release and a Newly Discovered Document Concerning the Life of Geoffrey Chaucer*, Speculum, 68 (January, 1993), 74-94.

From the above observations it appears to me that Cecily Chaumpaigne's release in the above memorandum should be considered to be the genuine version, and that this has nothing whatsoever to do with an added note of 'a rape' to be found in the close roll sent from the royal court. Not surprisingly the signed witnesses to that note comprised of Sir William de Beauchamp, King's Chamberlain and others of the court circle; John Clanvowe, William Nevill, John Philpot, and Richard Morel, all of these being members of that unprincipled clique who would willingly have assented to any action deemed likely to bring them greater royal favour. The Life-Records adds the following significant information: 'The single word (rape) in the Close Roll is the only word anywhere suggesting crime of any sort in the affair, and we must bear in mind that no one incurred legal responsibility for its use in the document, or undertook to prove its truth.' (*Life-Records*, p. 346)

(Chaucer / the Ploughman)

As in the closely linked examples of the Prioress and Second Nun; the Ploughman's identity is best determined from his closeness to the Parson: 'With hym ther was a Plowman, was his brother.'(*GP* 529) Such a close connection with the Parson is not only implied in a lack of physical description, but is also found in their identical acts of practical charity towards the more destitute amongst the neighbours: 'Ful looth were hym to cursen for his tithes,/ But rather wolde he yeven, out of doute, / Unto his povre parisshens aboute / Of his offryng and eek of his substaunce;' (GP 486-89) of the Parson's brother we are informed that: 'He wolde thresshe, and therto dyke and delve, / For Cristes sake, for every povre wight, / Withouten hire, if it lay in his might.' (*GP* 536-38)

(King Richard / the Miller)

The Miller personifies a powerful disposition of King Richard: 'At wrastlynge he wolde have alwey the ram.' (*GP* 548) He is also described as being a thief who charges three times his due for the services he provides: 'Wel koude he stelen corn and tollen thries; / And yet he hadde a thombe of gold, pardee.' (*GP* 62-63)

I consider this 'thombe of gold' detail to be of an added significant when it's considered with the above 'tollen thries;' it appears then to be a likely description of Richard's resorting to the royal signet-ring in order to circumvent the resistance of those who attempted to curtail his excessive spending: 'Beside Burley there was one other figure of the older generation who was a major influence on Richard. This was Michael de la Pole ... He had been placed in the household by parliament in 1381 to advise and counsel the young king and he had quickly won his charge's trust. On his appointment as chancellor he became one of Richard's most reliable lieutenants. He acquiesced in the king's use of the signet (ring) to move the great seal and abetted him in his efforts to evade parliamentary curbs on his expenditure.'[74] Such as the signet worn on the king's thumb would most likely have been fashioned out of 'gold,' and its use in the above deceitful manner could well have transferred large quantities of extra revenue (tollen thries) into the royal coffers.

(Chaucer / the Manciple)

The Manciple figures Chaucer's honesty and skill in household management: 'A gentil Maunciple was ther of a temple, / Of which achatours myghte take example / For to be wise in bynge of vitaille.' (*GP* 567-69) A warrant under the Privy Seal, 12 July 1389, had secured Chaucer's appointment as Clerk of the Works at Westminster, the Tower of London, and other castles, manors and lodges: 'Chaucer was to find labourers and set them to work, to provide the necessary materials, to make payments and to account by view of a controller …

---

[74] Saul, p. 117.

for the sale of branches and bark (offals) of trees purveyed for the king's works ... One difference in Chaucer's appointment being that he was to remain in office during his good behaviour, whereas his immediate predecessors had been appointed during pleasure ... His experience as controller of the customs helped to fit him for an office in which accounting played so important a part.'[75]

The significant lines in this Manciple presentation appear to be those that indicate a lord's need to retain servants that are capable of assisting him in his role as protector of his subjects should social misfortunes arise: 'Or lyve as scarsly as hym list desire; / And able for to helpen al a shire / In any caas that myghte falle or happe.' (*GP* 564-66) Being an outstanding example in his profession: 'This Manciple sette hir aller cappe,' *(GP* 586) his 'byynge of vitaille'(*GP* 569) caps that of all those others considered to be competent in estate management: 'To make hym lyve by his proper good / In honour dettelees (but if he were wood).' (*GP* 581-82)

Chaucer, in this portrayal of himself as the honest Manciple, could be anticipating the Host's later warning that the inebriated Richard / Cook aspect may in future seek revenge for the criticism of his drunkenness: 'But yet, Manciple, in feith thou

---

[75] Crow and Olson, Chaucer's <u>Life-Records</u>, Oxford, 1966. (pp. 412-13).

art to nyce, / Thus openly repreve hym of his vice. / Another day he wolle, peraventure, / Reclayme thee and brynge thee to lure; / I meene, he speke wole of smale thynges, / As for to pynchen at thy rekenynges, / That were nat honest, if it cam to preef.' (*Pro. MancT* 69-75). Being another aspect of King Richard, the Host would likewise have implied a future threatening of the Manciple with such a false accusation of dishonesty.

The Manciple's ironic and mocking response of fear following this comment has not found its better in all of the humour to be found in English literature: '"No," quod the Manciple, "that were a greet mescheef! / So myghte he lightly brynge me in the snare. / Yet hadde I levere payen for the mare / Which he rit on, than he sholde with me stryve. / I wol nat wratthen hym, also moot I thryve! / That that I spak, I seyde it in my bourde. / And wite ye what? I have heer in a gourde / A draghte of wyn, ye, of a ripe grape, / And right anon ye shul seen a good jape, / This Cook shal drynke therof, if I may. / Up peyne of deeth, he wol nat seye me nay."' (*Pro MancT* 76-86)

It's probably worth mentioning here that a similar royal threatening is to be found in King Henry II's attempts to such a 'greet mescheef' for Chaucer's 'hooly blissful martir.' (*GP* 17) That is Henry's own troublesome version of one who also demonstrated a greater love and obedience to God's

103

laws rather than to those of his sovereign: 'Henry began to make a series of unexpected demands for monies which he claimed were due to him from Thomas ... three barons - including William of Eynsford, who would hardly have supported the Archbishop who had excommunicated him if he thought Thomas in the wrong - stood surety.'[76]

(King Richard / the Reeve)

We are here introduced to the mad / 'wood' figure of Oswold the Reeve. This presentation of the Reeve recalls the Manciple lines of his ability to keep 'any lord that is in Engelond' within 'his propre good / In honour detelees ('but if he were wood.') The name 'Oswold' forms a compound of the Latin *ose* / full of; also the Anglo-Saxon word *wold* / wood. Significantly, Oswold's residence is described to be 'with grene trees yshadwed,' (*GP* 607) and he is himself described to be 'of carpenteris craft.' (*RvT* 3861)

A tale directed against the Reeve interests, the *Miller's Tale* is 'a legende and a lyf / Bothe of a carpenter and of his wyf;' (*MilT* 3141-42) within that tale the carpenter's woodness / madness is continually remarked upon: 'They tolden every man

[76] Loxton H., <u>Pilgrimage to Canterbury</u>, David & Charles Publishers, 1978, (p.45).

that he was wood;' (*MilT* 3833) 'Than he was holde wood in al the toun;' (*MilT* 3846) 'The man is wood, my leeve brother.' (*MilT* 3848) Being the instruments of the Reeve's later revenge on the Miller, the young clerks of his tale are both linked to the Reeve through the descriptions of their birth in a town 'highte Strother;' (*RvT* 4014) 'strowther' / to strew, to spread. Apparently this word 'strowther' could imply a 'wooded' area.

Furthermore, this Reeve pilgrim represents a later version of the earlier woodland Yeoman presentation. The Yeoman had accompanied the earlier twenty-year-old Squire, and it's specified that the Reeve has been in his master's employment 'Syn that his lord was twenty yeer of age.' (*GP* 601) The Yeoman's 'not head' (*GP* 109) and his 'cote and hood of grene,' (*GP* 103) being recalled in the Reeve's 'dokked hair' (*GP* 590) and his 'cote and hood.' (*GP* 612) The Yeoman's 'gay daggere / Harneised wel and sharp as point of spere,' (*GP* 113-14) having now been transformed into the Reeve's 'rusty blade.' (*GP* 618) Elsewhere we find that Chaucer describes the figure of 'Hate' to be 'lyk a wod woman ... ful foul and rusty.' (*Rom* 154 - 159). This Reeve disposition represents the hate-filled bloody tyranny of King Richard's final years on the throne: 'They were adrad of hym as of the deeth.' (*GP* 605)

It's not surprising that this Reeve figure is the greatest 'hinderance' to the desired Christian arrival of the pilgrims at Canterbury Cathedral: 'And evere he rood the hyndrest of oure route.' (*GP* 622) Here the word 'hyndrest' conveys an identical sense to that found in: 'Neither of us in love to hyndre oother;' (*KnT* 1135) or in: 'And hynderest hem, with thy translaciouns.' (*LGW F*. 250) I therefore take it that the above: 'And evere he rood the hyndreste of oure route,' (*GP* 622) is not intended to signify the presently accepted meaning of the Reeve being the lastly positioned amongst the pilgrims; here, rather than this the word 'hyndreste' indicates that King Richard's murderous and tyrannical actions present the greatest 'hinderance' to the possibility of his spiritual revival at the Canterbury shrine.

The following lines also explain why this Reeve's presence obstructs the pilgrimage's success: 'He koude better than his lord purchace. / Ful riche he was astored pryvely. / His lord wel koude he plesen subtilly, / To yeve and lene hym of his owene good, / And have a thank, and yet a cote and hood.' (*GP* 608-12) Even if this results in murderous tyranny in order to please his own extravagant 'lordly' disposition, the reality behind this Reeve sanctions the 'purchace' / expropriation of the estates belonging to his wealthier subjects;

and this is surely why he is also described to be 'of lawe expert and curious.' (*GP* 577)

Telling hints of the work's ongoing allegory also emerge in the following lines: 'This Reve sat upon a ful good stot / That was al pomely grey and highte Scot.' (*GP* 615-16) That is the Reeve is implied to be 'sitting' upon the grey / pale in colour peasantry, and this description will be recalled later in the *Friar's Tale* when, figured there as the impoverished widow, they are being robbed by that tale's somonour: 'Nay, olde stot, that is nat myn entente, / Quod this somonour, for to repente me / For any thing that I have had of thee. / I wolde I hade thy smok and every clooth!' (*FrT* 1630-33)

The closing connection with the next pilgrim: 'Of Northfolk was this Reve of which I telle, / Biside a toun men clepen Bawdeswell,' (*GP* 619-20) suggests that the naming of the Reeve's town as Bawdeswell / bawd - es - well prepares us to anticipate the next pilgrim figure of King Richard to be of a 'bawdy' disposition. Such a one as 'wolde suffer for a quart of wyn / A good felawe to have his concubyn / A twelf month, and excuse hym atte fulle.' (*GP* 649-51)

(King Richard / the Summoner)

Whereas the earlier Friar aspect of King Richard 'was an esy man to yeve penaunce;' (*GP*

223) this Summoner disposition is not to be trusted in his promises of having forgiven those he has previously cursed. Obviously Chaucer is not here attacking the Catholic Church's service of Absolution. Rather than this he is indicating the Summoner disposition's inability, regardless of his having received past monetary compensation, to forgive those he considered to have previously 'sinned' against his arbitrary rule: 'Of cursing oghte ech gilty man him drede, / For curs wol slee right as assoillyng savith, / And also war hym of a *Significavit.'* (*GP* 660-62) In other words those that had offended him should also be fearful of a *significavit* / of a future imprisonment.

Possibly the lines: 'And eek ye knowen wel how that a jay / Kan clepen Watte as wel as kan the pope,' (*GP* 642-43) connects this pilgrim with the earlier brilliance of such as the Reeve's 'cote and hood.' The vividness of the Summoner's apparel being hinted in the above 'jay:' O. Fr. *Jay* / *gay*; such colouring as is found in the gay / bright feathers of this woodland bird. The phrase: 'Kan clepen Watte' suggested that 'Watte' / Walter could be the name of King Richard's tailor; and I later found this to be historically correct, the name of his tailor had been Walter Rauf.'

Whereas the Friar's power of confession provided him with the necessary 'silver' required to arrange marriages 'of younge wommen at his

108

owene cost;' (*GP* 213) the money that this Summoner gained from 'absolutions' paid for the sexual favours of the young females within his parish: 'In daunger hadde he at his owene gise / The yonge girles of the diocise, / And knew hir conseil, and was al hir reed' (*GP* 663-65).

(King Richard / the Pardoner)

The previous masculine described Summoner pilgrim is accompanied by the effeminate Pardoner. This being another figure that demonstrates the purposeful contrasts to be found in these various pilgrims; such dispositions or aspects of personality as display contradictory struggle within the one totality.

The Pardoner's 'voys' is described to be 'as small as hath a goot;' (*GP* 688) and this is immediately seen to contrast with the Summoner's loud and deep voice: 'This Somonour bar to hym a stif burdoun; / Was nevere trompe of half so greet a soun.' (*GP* 674-75) As well as indicating a deep bass sound the word 'burdoun' also described a pilgrim's staff; it therefore seems more than likely that the 'stif burdoun' this Summoner 'bar / bare,' carried or uncovered to the Pardoner implies an erect penis. The allegorical sense here being that when the effeminate Pardoner aspect within King Richard's personality becomes sexually aroused he sings out for that penis firmness which in turn brings forth his masculine Summoner disposition: 'Ful loude he soong Com hider, love, to me!' (*GP* 672-73).

Another contrast between these two pilgrims is that the Pardoner represents a slightly soberer disposition than the drunken Summoner of whom it's declared: 'Wel loved he garleek, oynons, and eek lekes, / And for to drynken strong wyn, reed as blood.' (*GP* 634-35) To indicate this difference the earlier Summoner presentation had closed on the following: 'A garland hadde he set upon his heed, / As greet as it were for an ale-stake. / A bokeleer hadde he maad hym of a cake.' (*GP* 666-68) When the Pardoner later presents us with a near repeat of these lines: 'Heere at this alestake / I wol bothe drynke and eten of a cake,' (*Pro PardT* 321-22) Chaucer provides us with another example of his allegorical skills. Although the wording is but slightly different, I believe it's significant. Whereas the Summoner plays with his piece of bread instead of eating it: 'A bokeleer hadde he maad hym of a cake,' (*GP* 668) the Pardoner disposition eats his portion of cake / bread and however little this intake of food is it lower's his level of intoxication. Being that he eats his 'cake' as he drinks his alcohol the Pardoner retains a better capability to think 'upon som honest thing while that I drynke.' (Pro *PardT* 328)

110

Of course the level of sobriety is not solely dependant on the quantity or the strength of the alcohol consumed; it also bears a direct relationship to the lack of, or even to the type of food that has been absorbed before or during the drinking process. The Pardoner disposition is not therefore being hypocritical when he condemns the Summoner's drunkenness, and his fierce attack on that condition is shown in this criticism of this inebriated Summoner opposite: 'A lecherous thing is wyn, and dronkenesse / Is ful of stryvyng and of wrecchedness. / O dronke man, disfigured is thy face.' (*PardT* 549-51)

If only to increase the collection of what I consider are significant and interesting connections that have been drawn between the realities being depicted above; of course, I would geatly appreciate the time necessary to extend this study of the *General Prologue*. I believe that such linking patterns as I have presented above are meaningful to our forming a better understanding of the connecting allegorical framework to be found in both the *General Prologue* and in the *Tales*. However, as Chaucer has mentioned elsewhere, I too am forced to accept that I have 'God woot, a large feeld to ere, / And wayke been the oxen in my plough.' (*KnT* 886-87)

My ordering of the Tales
.

Knight - Miller - Reeve - Cook - Man of
Law - Squire - Franklin - Physcian -
Pardoner - Clerk - Merchant - Wife of Bath -
Friar - Summoner - Shipman - Prioress - Sir
Thopas - Melibee - Monk - Nun's Priest -
Second Nun - Canon's Yeoman –Manciple –
Parson

The Tales

The Knight's Tale

Chaucer's source for this tale is Boccaccio's *Teseida*; however, let us not forget that 'he handled his source freely, omitting much of Boccaccio's narrative and adding much of his own.'[77] Although the background formations may often be taken from the *Teseida*, the reading of Chaucer's specific allegorical sentence and the historical connections to be found in the *Knight's Tale* is my main concern. This will be the primary focus in my interpretations throughout my investigations into the tale.

The underlying 'signs and circumstances' to be found throughout the *Canterbury Tales* imply that the reality being allegorised here is the totality of Richard II's thoughts as this young king confronts those internal passions detering him from achieving personal and political maturity. Within the human psyche opposing tendencies often strive towards achieving a final resolution to perplexing questions. Whether it's the gods, the goddesses, the mythical heroes or the humans, that are here presented to be battling for supremacy, I consider such figures to be personifications of differing

---

[77] *Riverside*, p. 827.

psychological dispositions and inclinations within the young king's intellect.

In Greek mythology the Athenian state signified a well ordered form of government; that of Thebes conveyed the opposite of an administration constantly distressed by passion and the resultant civil agitation. Whereas Theseus of Athens displayed lawful rule; Creon of Thebes presented such a tyrannical disposition as incited social disorder. Within this tale the supportive gods and goddesses obliquely represent and direct the underlying rational or irrational psychological tendencies within the tale's leading human figures. Whereas Theseus implies the best notions of statehood within King Richard's intellect: 'the porche (that is to seyn, a gate of the toun of Athenis, there as philosophris hadden hir congregacioun to desputen) - thilke porche brought somtyme olde men, ful dirke in hir sentences;' (*Bo*. Book V, Metrum 4, 1-5) the Creon disposition figures the opposite intemperate rule of Thebes: 'Al th'assage of Thebes and the care; / For herof ben ther maked bookes twelve.' (*Tr*. Book II, 107-8) In this *Knight's Tale* these opposites depict contrasting responses within King Richard's psyche as being fluctuations between the 'wisdom and chivalrie' (*KnT* 865) of Theseus and the passionate 'ire and iniquitee' (*KnT* 940) of his opposing Creon of Thebes moods. In order that we understand and are thereafter better able to unravel the hidden historical events being implied within the tale, Chaucer has ensured that the changes he has inserted into his version of the tale are often set within significant indicators of a contemporary time scale.

In early 1382 King Richard had married Anne of Bohemia; although at that time legally at liberty to run his private affairs without outside intervention, being fully aware of his susceptibility to the flattery of the unprincipled favourites at his court, the powerful party of nobles that attempted to direct him into a more competent rule were unwilling to renounce the control they had established during the reign's minority years. Historically known as the Appellant Lords this group, headed by the king's uncle Thomas of Gloucester, were probably correct to be so concerned. Following the recent Peasants' Revolt of 1381 they feared that if the king's extravagances were not curtailed such a plague of social disorders as the country had lately experienced could return. Probably the excessively proud young king became greatly angered by what he considered to be this unwarranted containment of his personal freedom; and he seems to have become encouraged by the flatterers at his court to regard this as being treasonable actions against his royal prerogative.

Later in the reign the appellants believed themselves forced to separate the young king from such influences as they considered to be foolishly leading their sovereign into wasteful and therefore highly dangerous social improprieties. They formed the Appellant Council and held power for a little longer than twelve months. During that time they sought to lead their sovereign into a better perception and compliance with his royal duties. On May 3, 1389, King Richard effectively countered the restrictions they had imposed on his power, and in so doing he established governmental control; his pledge of administering social justice in the future being accompanied by the necessary sworn oaths of forgiveness towards the former appellant opposition. An eminent American scholar, Johnstone Parr, believed he detected parallels between this period of King Richard's reign and the *Knight's Tale*. Most importantly he considered that the line 'to have with certain contrees alliaunce,' (*KnT* 2973) was likely to be an allusion to the peace negotiations that in 1389 took place between England, France, Spain and Scotland. Secondly, that the *Knight's Tale* also contained references of King Richard's 1390 Smithfield tournament in London.[78]

Chaucer's mention of the tempest that raged at the time of Queen Hipolyta's arrival in her new homeland: 'The tempest at hir hoom-comynge,'

---

[78] Parr, Johnstone, *The Date and Revision of Chaucer's Knight's Tale*, PMLA 60, 1945, (pp. 307-24).

(*KnT* 884) is not to be found in Boccaccio's original version of the tale. It was not therefore unreasonable for another reader to consider that its inclusion into Chaucer's *Knight's Tale* could be an allusion to a contemporary event: 'Lowes sees here a reference to the storm that destroyed the ship that brought Anne of Bohemia, then fiancée of Richard II, to England on 18 December 1381.'[79] I would agree with Lowes that it's very likely this storm signified that specific tempest; and, further to this, in my opinion that Chaucer included it into his tale in order to provide an historical starting date for his version of the *Teseida*.

It could be that both 'Ypolita, / The faire, hardy queene of Scithia (*KnT* 868) ... 'And eek hir yonge suster Emelye,'(*KnT* 871) imply the background historical reality of Queen Anne. Paul Piehler describes such historical inclusions rather well: 'The figure of Beatrice, however, has a significance in the development of the visionary potential that goes beyond the aspects we have been describing. Previously, the *potentia* had been based on the figure of a god or goddesss, or the closely related figure of the allegorical abstraction. Now it begins to manifest itself in the form of a person encountered in the poet's everyday experience, or in a figure of history ... Already in the *Romance of the*

---

[79] *Riverside*, p. 826.

Rose it is possible to see the lineaments of the lady behind the abstract figures and concrete symbols that represent various aspects of her effect on the dreamer. Nonetheless, the great step towards modern conceptions was clearly Dante's figure of Beatrice, after which allegories based on concrete personalities became frequent.'[80]

The Theban women said to interrupt the homeward journey of Theseus towards Athens: a 'compaignye of ladyes, tweye and tweye, / Ech after oother clad in clothes blake,' (*KnT* 898-99) are probably to be understood as being such 'abstract figures' as signify the 'wo and ... distresse' (*KnT* 919) that indicates the remnants of a dark Theban temper within the young king's intellect. Such figures as represent a dangerous angry passion that must be surpressed before the opposing Athenian / Theseus disposition of good government is able to regain the conduct of King Richard's political actions.

Differently to his source in Boccaccio, Chaucer locates his 'Temple of the goddesse Clemence' (*KnT* 928) outside rather than inside the walls of Athens; that is, King Richard must master his revengeful feelings towards the appellants before his Theseus disposition can be described as having returned home to Athens 'with laurer

---

[80] Piehler, pp. 140-142.

crowned as a conquerour.' (*KnT* 1027) The mythological Minotaur, a representative of mankind's animal nature having broken free from the restrictions of rational human values, ensures that the Theseus aspect of mind will now carry into his battle against Thebes the emblem of a previous victory over such an inner malevolent passion; possibly such a passionate anger as he had held towards those involved in the Peasant's Revolt is being inferred: 'And by his baner born is his penoun / Of gold ful riche, in which ther was ybete / The Mynotaur, which that he wan in Crete.' (*KnT* 978-80)

Having secured his victory in the initial battle against the Theban-like causes of psychological disruption, King Richard's Athenian disposition 'stille in that feeld ... took al nyght his reste.' (*KnT* 1003) The return of a Theban form of hostility towards the appellants remains a threat however, and that potential danger is figured in the discovery of Arcite and Palamon amongst the slain Thebans: 'Nat fully quyke, ne fully dede they were. / The heraudes knewe hem best in special / As they that weren of the blood roial / Of Thebes, and of sustren two yborn. / Out of the taas the pilours han hem torn, / And han hem carried softe unto the tente / Of Theseus.' (*KnT* 1015-22) From here onwards in the tale the future peace of King Richard's reign will depend on how firmly this Theseus / Athenian disposition of mind retains mastery over these two remaining 'blood royal' knights of Theban disorder. His initial reaction to their discovery is undoubtedly the correct response: 'He ful soone hem sente / To Atthenes, to dwellen in prisoun / Pepetuelly – he nolde no raunsoun.' (*KnT* 1022 -24) The need of such an Athenian-like firmness regarding the imprisonment of the two young Thebans being highly significant to our fuller understanding of the tale's allegory.

Unaware of the tale's figurative dimension, and then probably influenced by his reading of the Knight's character to be that of a ruthless mercenary, Terry Jones failed to understand the reasoning behind Theseus' refusal to grant clemency to the two young Thebans, and because of this omission he incorrectly considered the *Knight's Tale* to be 'the antithesis of largess - that special generosity which was so crucial a part of true knighthood ... In the *Knight's Tale* this is never mentioned. In the *Teseida* Teseo is careful to distribute largess after his successful assault on Thebes ... He had his men bring him whatever they had won, and he freely and generously divided their shares amongst his knights ... The Knight makes no mention of this. He stresses, instead, that Theseus refused to allow any ransom for Palamon and Arcite - which was in itself an act contrary to the spirit of largess - unless accompanied by some sort of compensation to those of his men who had caught them.'[81]

On seeing Emelye from the 'prison' of their captivity: 'She gadereth floures, party white and rede, / To make a subtil garland for hire hede; / And as an aungel hevenysshly she soong;' (*KnT* 1053-1055) there follows a heated debate between Palamon and Arcite, such a difference of opinion as depict contrary forms of loving within King Richard's psyche. Whereas Palamon declares: 'To love my lady, whom I love and serve, / And evere shal til that myn herte sterve;' (*KnT* 1143-4) the Arcite disposition's counters with: 'For paramour I loved hire first er thow. / What wiltow seyn? Thou woost nat yet now / Wheither she be a woman or goddesse! / Thyn is affeccioun of hoolynesse, / And myn is love as to a creature.' (*KnT* 1155-59)

Arcite's response to Palamon's anguished cry: 'Why cridestow? Who hath thee doon offence? / For Goddes love, taak al in pacience / Oure prisoun, for it may noon oother be. / Fortune hath yeven us this adversitee. / Som wikke aspect or disposicioun / Of Saturn, by som constellecioun, / Hath yeven us this although we hadde it sworn; / So stood the hevene whan that we were born;'(*KnT* 1083-1090) identifies further the unifying closeness that these two share within the tale. Not only are

---

[81] Jones, Terry, (p. 162-63).

they 'of sustern two yborn,' they are also described as being 'cosyn and thy brother.' (*KnT* 1131) They are now also described to have been born under the same constellation, one in which Saturn displays its malefic influence. The date of King Richard's birth, January 6th 1367 was in that month that the constellation Capricorn had its transit under the planet's greater influence, from December 22 to January 19^{th,}

The Palamon aspect gives his service to 'Venus, goddesse of love;' (*KnT* 1904) and Arcite deifies 'Mars armypotente.' (*KnT* 1982) The tale's figure of Emelye venerates 'Dyane the chaste.' (*KnT* 2051) Precisely what these influences denote are vividly portrayed upon the walls of their respective temples. When lacking opposing restrictions Mars figures 'open werre, with woundes al bibledde; / Contek, with blody knyf and sharp manace;' (*KnT* 2002-3) Venus signifies 'festes, instrumentz, caroles, daunces, / Lust and array.' (*KnT* 1931-2) The countering Diana influence honoured by Emily signifies 'shamefast chastitee.' (*KnT* 2055) At this stage in the tale the figure of Theseus is described to be a compound of the warrior Mars and the chaste Diana influences: 'After Mars he serveth now Dyane.' (*KnT* 1682)

The arrival of Perotheus in Athens is described to be that of a Theban disposition that 'loved wel Arcite, / And hadde hym knowe at

Thebes yeer by yere.' (*KnT* 1202-03) His entrance into the tale signals a return of an unruly Theban influence into the Mars / Diana psyche of King Richard. This dangerous intervention ushers a mood of frivolity into the moral stance that the tale's figure of Theseus had previously possessed: 'A worthy duc that highte Perotheus, / That felawe was unto duc Theseus / Syn thilke day that they were children lite, / Was come to Atthenes his felawe to visite, / And for to pleye as he was wont to do.' (*KnT* 1191-95) The two important pointers here being 'children lite;' and 'to pleye as he was wont to do.' Such a description confirms the 'hellish' nature of this emerging force, Chaucer will now presents us with a significant literary representation not to be found in Boccaccio's tale: 'So wel they lovede, as olde bookes sayn, / That whan that oon was deed, soothly to telle, / His felawe wente and sought hym doun in helle - / But of that storie list me nat to write.' (*KnT* 1196-1201)

This dark Theban influence of Perotheus is powerful enough to persuade the King Richard compound of Mars and Diana to revise his earlier decision regarding Arcite's perpetual imprisonment. The previous: 'he wolde no raunson,' (*KnT* 1024) is now changed into the granting of Arcite's freedom 'without any raunsoun.' (*KnT* 1205) Although on his freedom banished from Athens: if 'he were caught back it was accorded thus, / That with a swerd he sholde lese his heed.' (*KnT* 1214-15) The disguised Arcite returns to Athens under the assumed name of Philostrate = philo / lover; strate / stratagem, from Lat. *strategema*; an artifice in war, a trick by which the enemy can be deceived. In this Philostrate disguise and his show of good behaviour Arcite pretends that he is the very opposite of his true nature. This cloaked Theban aspect of mind is soon able to convince Theseus that he is 'gentil of condicioun,' (*KnT* 1431) and with such a deception he secures a close personal acceptance: 'Theseus hath taken hym so neer / That of his chamber he made hym a squire.' (*KnT* 1439-40) Not unexpectedly this 'blood royal' figure of Thebes expresses his utter contempt for such a forced compliance of goodness: 'Now highte I Philostrate, noght worth a myte.' (*KnT* 1558)

Palamon the remaining captive Theban secures his freedom when Theseus his Athenian guard is described to have become intoxicated. The implication here being that King Richard has now become so enamoured with a Theban recklessness that the previous Mars / Diana compound is no longer able to maintain custody over this previously suppressed Theban disposition: 'For he hadde yeve his gayler drynke so / Of a clarree maad of a certeyn wyn, / With nercotikes and opie of Thebes fyn, / That al that nyght, thogh that men wolde him shake, / The gayler sleep; he myghte nat awake.' (*KnT*

1470-74) No longer will King Richard allow himself to consider the counselling of those that had aided him through the Athenian period of his Mars / Diana discretion.

A highly significant detail not found in the source material: 'Boccaccio says only that the action took place when the moon was in Sagittarius,'[82] is when Palamon's escape is specified to be 'In the seventhe yer, of May / The thridde nyght.' (*KnT* 1462-63) In order to create an denial of this date being a rather obvious reference to King Richard's political countering and defeating of the appellant power in 1389, the seeming falsehood of it being found in an earlier work has been carefully bracketed by Chaucer for our attention: ('as olde bookes seyn, / That al this storie tellen moore pleyn.') (*KnT* 1463-4)

The interval from the tale's implied commencement to that of Palamon's escape on the third of May seven years later is now seen to correspond with the historical interval from King Richard and Queen Anne's wedding on January 20th 1382, to the third of May 1389; that is, to the year and the exact date when King Richard overthrew the power of the appellants: 'At a council meeting in the Marcolf chamber at Westminster on 3 May he announced his assumption of personal responsibility

---

[82] *Riverside*, p. 832.

for the governance of the realm … On the next day he dismissed the ministers imposed on him by the Appellants.'[83] Furthermore, the grand tournament arranged by Theseus is described to follow 'this fifty wykes, fer ne ner' (*KnT* 1850) from this May 3 date; this being a readily recognisable event that complements the timing of King Richard's grand tournament at Smithfield in 1390: 'Now we should be placing a definite limitation upon Chaucer's poetic imagination were we to suppose that he could not write these parts of his poem without having recently witnessed a tournament at Smithfield; yet there is much in favour of the theory that the tournament of 1390 is reflected in the *Knight's Tale*.'[84]

I would press the inclusion of this tournament further; that Chaucer has not only inserted into his version of Boccaccio's tale what Parr described as being 'elements of medieval realism and an excellent piece of belated news-reporting;'[85] the main reason for his having done so was to provide us with a greater awareness regarding the historical background that underlies this tale's allegory. Not only do we now have the above period of seven years from King Richard / Queen Anne's marriage to the above mentioned May 3, 1389; there has also

---

[83] Saul, p. 203,

[84] Parr, J., (p. 318).

[85] Ibid. p. 323.

126

been added another year; one that takes us to 1390, the year that King Richard's held his tournament at Smithfield.

I disagree with Parr's interpretation of the following lines: 'I do vengeance and pleyn correccioun, / Whil I dwelle in the signe of the leoun.' (*KnT* 2461-62) Although he correctly connected the significance of Saturn's influence within the planetary tables of dates he provided in his essay, I believe he was mistaken when taking the above 'vengeance' and 'pleyn correccioun' as being allusions of two separate historical incidents. The first of these he read to be the 'vengeance' of the appellants against those who had so traitorously misdirected the young king; the second to the 'pleyn correccioun' found in King Richard's 1389 dismissal of these same appellants: 'The kingdom was legitimately forced to nullify the Council of Regency and accept Richard as king. The time for "pleyn correccioun," Richard and his friends might have said, had come.'[86]

Considering it to be a depiction of King Richard's fluctuating intellectual considerations, my allegorical reading of this tale is that Saturn's passage in the 'signe of the leoun' results in the king himself being incited with varying degrees of 'vengeance and pleyn correccioun.' When

---

[86] Ibid., p. 314.

possessing such malevolence Saturn's 'looking is the fader of pestilence;' (*KnT* 2469) and this 'looking' can then bring about 'the ruyne of the hye halles.' (*KnT* 2463) However, as Parr observes Saturn's influence in this phase was rapidly diminishing at that time and would soon be no more: 'Saturn passed from the sign of the Lion on August 15, 1389;'[87] this weaker period of Saturn's passage is now intended to indicate a time when King Richard seemed to have put aside all thoughts of vengeance, and instead of conflict he had become persuaded to form a peaceful alliance with the former appellants.

Whereas the earlier union of the Mars / Diana dispositions within the Theseus intellect had inspired his Athenian rule; his later acceptance of Palamon, and with this his compelling of the Emelye / Diana disposition to take him as her husband and lord: 'You shul of youre grace upon hym rewe, / And taken hym for housbonde and for lord,' (*KnT* 3080-81) implies the threat that this powerful Venus influence within King Richard's psyche could eventually eclipse his chaste Diana aspect. Such a significant psychological movement within the earlier Theseus disposition of Mars and Diana may results in the directing of King Richard's thoughts towards a Palamon / Venus

---

[87] Ibid. p. 314.

aspect of mind. Towards a goddess that, in return for her securing him lordship over the chaste figure of Emelye, Palamon had promised her that he would 'holden werre alwey with chastitee.' (*KnT* 2236)

Earlier in the tale Theseus had declared his awareness of the God of Love's power: 'How mighty and how greet a lord is he!' (*KnT* 1786) He had then also possessed the ability to recall the folly that accompanies such a 'hot' service: 'A man moot ben a fool, or yong or oold – / I woot it by myself ful yore agon, / For in my tyme a servant was I oon.' (*KnT* 1812-14) At that time he could compare and assess the wisdom of pardoning those 'that been in repentaunce and drede' (*KnT* 1776) with a necessary refusal of amnesty to 'a proud despitous man / That wol meyntene that he first bigan.' (*KnT* 1777-78) He is now unable to consider the dangers that confronts his peace following the release of these two 'yonge knyghtes proud;' (*KnT* 2598) and because of this he grants Palamon his freedom without the essential precondition that he has dispensed with that 'first began' against his Athenian rule. Clearly his initial decision of perpetual imprisonment remained the correct response to 'al hir bisy torment, and hir fir.' (*KnT* 2320)

Notwithstanding the dangers that may follow the Theseus acceptance of granting freedom to the

Palamon aspect, the tale's closing lines express the Knight's desires for a secure continuation of the Mars and chaste Diana compound that had initially inspired Theseus: 'Bitwixen hem was maad anon the bond / That highte matrimoigne or marriage. / By al the conseil and the baronage. / And thus with alle blisse and melodye / Hath Palamon ywedded Emelye. / And God, that al this wyde world hath wroght, / Sende hym his love that hath it deere abought; / For now is Palamon in alle wele, / Lyvynge in blisse, in richesse, and in heele, / And Emelye hym loveth so tenderly, / And he hire serveth so gentilly, / That nevere was ther no word hem bitwene / Of jalousie or any oother teene.' (*KnT* 3094-3106)

The Miller's Prologue

The Narrator introduces the next tales, those told by the the Miller and the Reeve, with a warning of the vulgarity that they are likely to contain: 'And therefore every gentil wight I preye, / For Godds love, demeth nat that I seye / Of yvel entente, but for I moot reherce / Hir tales alle, be they better or werse, / Or ells falsen som of my mateere. / and therefore, whoso list it nat yheere, / Turne over the leef and chese another tale; / For he shal fynde ynowe, grete and smale, / Of storial thyng that toucheth gentillesse, / And eek moralitee and

130

hoolynesse. / Blameth nat me if that ye chese amys. / The Millere is a cherl; ye knowe wel this. / So was the Reve eek and othere mo, / And harlotrie they tolden bothe two.' (*MilPro*3171-3184)

I believe that Chaucer eventually came to regret having been so licentious in his condemnation of the one he was attempting to correct in these tales: 'Thyng that is seyd is seyd, and forth it gooth, / Though hym repente, or be hym nevere so looth. / He is his thral to whom that he hath sayd / A tale of which he is now yvele apayd.' (*MancT* 355-358) The *Parson's Tale* also contains an expression of this same guilt: 'For as seith Salomon, "The amyable tonge is the tree of lyf" – that is to seyn, of lyf espiritueel – and soothly, a deslavee tonge sleeth the spirites of hym that repreveth and eek of hym that is repreved. / Loo, what seith Seint Augustyn: "Ther is nothing so lyk the develes child as he that ofte chideth;" Seint Paul seith eek, "The servant of God bihoveth nat to chide."'(*ParsT* 628-29)

Professor Robertson described how the tradition of rebuke was most advantageously expressed: 'The lover is first advised to be generous, not in the manner satirized by Ovid, to the lady of his desire, but to everyone ... The lover is advised to be humble, respectful to God and to His saints ... With reference to speech, he is urged never to disparage anyone. On the other hand, he should not praise the wicked, but should admonish them privately, or, if they persist in wickedness, abandon their company altogether.'[88] It's not therefore surprising that Chaucer, when taking leave of this work, stresses his condemnation of 'the tales of Caunterbury, thilke that sownen into synne.' (*Riverside*, p. 328) By this means he appears to be stressing the sinful manner of his presentation of such tales as these next two, and those 'othere mo' of such a nature as are to be found in this Canterbury series.

The Miller's Tale

This tale's allegory covers a later historical period to that indicated by the Knight in his tale; however, we immediately come to understand that it has retained the allegorical structure of conflict between different aspects of King Richard's psyche. As could have been predicted from our reading of the *Knight's Tale*, the vigorous Venus temperament has vanquished the chaste Diana disposition: 'Thus may ye seen that wisdom ne richesse, / Beautee ne sleighte, strengthe ne hardynesse, / Ne may with Venus holde champartie, / For as hir list the world than may she gye / Lo, alle thise folk so caught

---

[88] Robertson, p. 416.

were in hir las, / Til they for wo ful ofte seyde "allas!"'(*KnT* 1947-52)

The previous tale's central figure of Theseus has now been replaced by the doting carpenter: 'A riche gnof' that 'hadde wedded newe a wyf, / Which he lovede moore than his lyf.' (*MilT* 3221-22) The previous tale's victorious Palamon disposition is here divided between the Venus inspired contraries of 'hende Nicholas' (*MilT* 3199) and 'joly Absolon.' (*MilT* 3348) The aggressive sexual directness with which Nicholas pursues Alison: he 'heeld hire harde by the haunchebones / And seyde, "Lemman, love me al atones,"' (*MilT* 3279-80) is set against the timidity of Absolon's loving: 'This joly Absolon, / Hath in his herte swich a love-longynge / That of no wyf took he noon offrynge; / For he wolde noon.' (*MilT* 3348-51) It appears to be implied here that the doting King Richard, when he is in this Absolon disposition, even rejects the 'offrynges' of the various 'wives' that were attendant at his court.

We are informed that Nicholas is: 'A poure scoler, / Hadde lerned art, but al his fantasye / Was turned for to lerne astrologye.' (*MilT* 3190-3193) King Richard's presence is also hinted in Absolon's golden locks: 'Crul was his heer, and as the gold it shoon, / And strouted as a fanne large and brode.' (*MilT* 3314-15) This description recalls the golden haired Emetreus of the previous tale: 'His crispe

133

heer lyk rynges was yronne, / And that was yelow, and glytered as the sonne.' (*KnT* 2165-66) Contemporary accounts of the young King Richard often compared him to the biblical figure of Absolon: 'All those who commented on his appearance were agreed on what they call his "beauty;" writing near the beginning of the reign John Gower described him as the "most beautiful of kings" and "the flower of boys;" some fifteen years later Maidstone declared him to be "as handsome as Paris" and "as gracious as Absolom." In an obituary notice Adam Usk claimed that he was as beautiful as Absolon.'[89]   Whereas Queen Anne appeared to have underlined the previous tale's descriptions and presence of Emelye: 'Hir yellow heer was broyded in a tresse / Bihynde hir bak, a yerde long, I gesse;' (KnT 1049-50) this tale's portrayal of the carpenter's 'joly colt' (*MilT* 3263) provides us with telling hints of the passage of time and with this of Queen Isabel's presence. Perhaps ironically, the earlier Prioress detail that she 'was nat undergrowe' (*GP* 156) is recalled in the description of the carpenter's 'yonge wyf' being as 'long as a mast.' (*MilT* 3264) Her 'fair forheed; / It was almoost a spanne brood, I trowe,' (*GP* 154-55) may be recalled in this 'youge wyf's' 'filet brood of silk.' (*MilT* 3243) The Prioress's 'brooch of gold' (*GP*

---

[89] Saul, (pp. 451-52).

160) in this wife's brooch being 'as brood as is the boos of a bokeler.' (*MilT* 3266) Such lines as 'Therto she koude skippe and make game, / As any kyde or calf folwynge his dame,' (*MilT* 3259-60) definitely implies her childhood.

Nicholas spends his days studying astrology and his nights playing a harp-like instrument until 'Al the chambre rong.' (*MilT* 3215) The funding of his friends and the rent of those who farm his lands: 'his freendes fyndyng and his rente,' (*MilT* 3220) maintaining him in this state of his bliss. Manuscripts then being both rare and costly suggests that such an allegorical identity as I propose best explains how Nicholas possesses so many valuable astrological items; such as 'his Almageste, and bookes grete and smale, / His astrelabie, longynge for his art, / His augrym stones layen faire apart.' (*MilT* 3208-13)

This tale's figure of Absolon implies the murderous tyranny of King Richard's final years on the throne, and with this comes a pointer to his confiscation of such as those lands that were previously owned by the appellants: 'Wel koude he laten blood, and clippe and shave, / And maken a chartre of lond or aquitaunce.' (*MilT* 3326-27) Probably the word 'clippe' carries such a meaning as today's phrase: 'to clip his wings;' 'shave' indicating the dire poverty of Richard's subjects. That final tyrannous period of his rule also seem to be implied in: 'Somtyme, to shewe his lightnesse and maistrye, / He pleyeth Herodes upon a scaffold hye.' (*MilT* 3383-84)

The songs sung by the sexually aroused Nicholas disposition imply what will be the tale's allegorical direction: 'And *Angelus ad virginem* he song; / And after that he song the Kynges Noote.' (*MilT* 3216-17) Both of these titles provide ingenious clues to the tale's theme, and of King Richard's hidden presence: *Angelus ad virginem* / the angel to the virgin, implying the harp playing and therefore 'angel-like' king's dilemma of having married a seven-year-old child whose virginity he was to respect until she arrived at puberty. The 'Kynges Noote' being a rather obvious indication of the kingly presence; 'note' from the Latin *nota*, an identifying mark. The various unsatisfactory attempts to find originals of these two songs are further examples of the difficulties that confront those attempting to construct a non-allegorical reading of the tale.

The many compound words to be found within the tale advances our awareness of the allegorical theme: 'She was a prymerole, a piggesnye, / For any lord to leggen in his bedde, / Or yet for any good yeman to wedde.' (*MilT* 3268-70) I take it that these terms: 'prymerole' and 'piggesnye,' are meant to indicate the Miller's impression of Alison's erotic qualities: 'pryme /

role' being a compound of 'prime' / the best; 'role' signifying such up and down rolling movements as take place during sexual intercourse. The hidden reality behind the figure of Alison is considered to be a 'prime roll' for 'any lord;' or for a 'good yeman' as this tale's carpenter, to 'leggen in his bedde.' The following *Reeve's Tale* of revenge against the Miller disposition, informs us that the tale's miller has a wife that's described to be 'wel ynorissed and a mayde, / To saven his estaat of yomanrye.' (*RvT* 3948-49)

As the description 'pig-eyed' applies to small and deeply set eyes, the above 'pigges / nye' implies that Absolon has 'kist hir nether ye;' this probably being an obscene punning on her deeply set 'nether ye.' (*MilT* 3852) Our deciphering of such as these composite words present us with the best possible explanation of the carpenter's alarm as nightime approaches:

> What! Nicholay! what, how! looke adoun.
> Awak, and thenk on Cristes passioun!
> I crouche thee from elves and fro wightes.`
> Therwith the night-spel seyde he anon-rightes
> On foure halves of the hous aboute,
> And on the thresshfold of the dore withoute:
> Jesu Crist and seinte Benedight,
> Blesse this hous from every wikked wight,

For nyghtes verye, the white pater-noster!
Where wentestow, seinte Petres soster?
(*MilT* 3477-3486)

The very thought of evening brings a mood of sexual arousal into the carpenter's psyche, and along with this comes his increasing awareness that a powerful and lustful mood is displacing the soberer disposition that he is attempting to suppress. Fearing the consequences of this he warns his Nicholas disposition to 'looke adoun,' probably towards his rising penis, and by so doing try to resist the growing feelings of such an unholy passion towards his child bride. In order to protect her from the wickedness that now threatens her virginity he encourages Nicholas to recall how Christ had suffered for our moral salvation. Not only does he cry out for Christ's assistance in this matter, but also for that of Saint Benedight; this 'Benedight' is correct, not the now accepted to be Benedict. 'Benedight' being another of this tale's compound words: *bene* / good; *dight* / sexual intercourse. *'Bene'* in the sense of the carpenter disposition's willingness to wait until his wife arrives at puberty before such an act takes place; 'dighte' should not present us with any interpretive difficulty: 'Was for t'espye wenches that he dighte.' (*WBT* 398) 'And lete hir lecchour dighte hire al the nyght.' (*WBT* 767). In his desperate attempt to avoid the immoral act that's about to take place, the carpenter also pleads assistance from what was then accepted to be Oxford's patron saint of devout virgins: 'Help us, Seinte Frydeswyde!' (*MilT* 3449) Significantly, this tale's 'riche gnof' of a carpenter is described to be 'dwellynge at Oxenford.'

If we keep to the sexual theme that I have suggested our understanding of the above 'verye' (*MilT* 3485) should not be troublesome: 'The meaning is uncertain. The best suggestion is "against the evil spirits of the night" possibly the mysterious *verye* is a derivative or a corruption of OE *we(ar)g* "evil spirit."'[90] Taking it to be another of Chaucer's compound words I believe that this compound neatly divides into 'ver' and 'ye:' a combination that also explains the above mentioned 'white pater-noster.' 'Ver' from the Latin *viridis* / green, the quality of greeness / verdancy: 'With newe grene, of lusty Ver the prime;' (*TC* I, 157) 'ye' being the earlier Anglo-Saxon form of 'you;' as in 'Ye goon to Caunterbury.' (*GP* 769) The carpenter's obvious problem being that night-time generates a 'greeness' in his 'white *pater-noster* / white our father / white penis;' and this 'greeness' threatens the virginity of his child-bride.

Figuratively understood the word 'white' signifies such virtue as is described in the

---

[90] *Riverside*, p. 846.

following: 'Right so was faire Cecilie the white / Ful swift and bisy evere in good werkynge.' (*SNT* 115-16) His having till that time resisted such an immoral sexual act with his child bride, the carpenter's *pater-noster* can be said to have retained a state of whiteness / of purity. This *pater-noster* euphemism for the penis is also hinted later when Nicholas, John and Alison, encourage it to 'climb' into an erection: '"Now, *Pater-noster*, clom!" seyde Nicholay, / And "Clom!" quod John, and "Clom!" seyde Alisoun.' (*MilT* 3638-39) Mistakenly glossed as meaning 'hush' by previous readers of the tale, when taken within such a figurative interpretation this 'clom' is immediately seen to be a shortened form of 'clomben / climbing.' A word that's repeated in full later in the tale when the carpenter; Nicholas and Alison, 'climb' up the ladder into the loft: 'And shortly, up they clomben alle thre.' (*MilT* 3636)

Probably the carpenter's comparison of his wife to 'seinte Petres soster' recalls Christ's censuring of Saint Peter for his placing of wordly matters on a higher level than the spiritual: 'But when he had turned about and looked on his disciples, he rebuked Peter, saying "Get thee behind me, Satan: for thou savourest not the things that be of God, but the things that be of men."'[91] By this

---

[91] <u>Saint Mark</u>, Chapter 8, verse 33)

reference to her as 'seinte Petres soster' the carpenter is preparing to blame his wife for the act of sexual depravity that's about to take place; he is implying her to be his tempting female version of Saint Peter.

An essential precondition before Nicholas and Alison can achieve their sexual union of bliss is a drunken sleep-filled stupor within the watchful carpenter disposition: 'This carpenter goth doun, and comth ageyn, / And broghte of myghty ale a large quart; / And whan that ech of hem had dronke his part, / This Nicholas his dore faste shette, / And doun the carpenter by hym he sette.' (*MilT* 3496-3500) The consequence of his ale drinking being that 'The dede sleep, for wery bisynesse, / Fil on this carpenter right, as I gesse.' (*MilT* 3643-44) Following this Nicholas and Alison: 'Withouten wordes mo they goon to bedde, / Ther as the carpenter is wont to lye.' (*MilT* 3650-51)

Other compound words implied in the tale being such as when Gervays the blacksmith greets Absolon with his: 'What eyleth yow? Som gay gerl, God it woot, / Hath broght yow thus upon the viritoot.' (*MilT* 3769-70) 'Ger / vays:' suggests the Latin. *gyrus* / a circle: such as is to be found in the naming of the ger-falcon from its 'circling' flight; 'ger' being added here to form a compound with 'vays / ways.' The implication of this being that the figure of 'Gervays' is to be taken as an aspect that circles between the various dispositions within King Richard's psyche. Another word that has generated a great deal of critical confusion being the above 'viritoot.' (*Riverside*, p. 848) This word I take to be a compound of *ver* / *viri* / green; 'toot' being closely allied word to 'tout' or 'teten' / a projection. Such as is found in 'His ton toteden out, as he the londe treddede.'[92] The Gervays disposition is obviously admonishing Absolon for allowing 'som gay gerl' to bring a 'viri toot / green projection' into what had previously been his 'white *pater-noster.*'

The Reeve's Prologue

Following the previous tale's completion we find that the Reeve, against whose interest the Miller's theme of 'nightes verye, the white pater-noster' was directed, replies with a frank admission of his own 'aged' disposition and with it his possession of a 'grene tayl:' 'We olde men, I drede, so fare we: / Til we be roten, kan we nat be rype; / We hoppen alwey whil that the world wol pype. / For in oure wyl ther stiketh evere a nayl, / To have an hoor heed and a grene tayl, / As hath a leek; for thogh oure might be goon, / Oure wyl desireth folie evere in oon.' (*MilT* 3874-80)

---

[92]Barr, Helen, (p. 79).

When the Reeve momentarily shifts into a consideration of those other follies that exist in the embers of his old-age: 'Foure gleedes han we, which I shal devyse - Avauntyng, liyng, anger, coveitise; / Thise foure sparkles longen unto eelde;' (*Pro RvT* 3883-85) it becomes obvious that the Host disposition of King Richard is immediately troubled by an awareness of their significance to his own behaviour: 'Whan that oure Hoost hadde herd this sermonyng, / He gan to speke as lordly as a kyng. / He seide, "What amounteth al this wit? / The devel made a reve for to preche, / ... Sey forth thy tale, and tarie nat the tyme. / Lo Depeford, and it is half-wey pryme! / Lo Grenewych, ther many a shrewe is inne!' (*Pro RvT* 3900-07) Notice two significant allegorical indicators in the passage; firstly, 'He gan to speke as lordly as a kyng;' secondly, the direct reference to Greenwich that part of London believed to contain Chaucer's living quarters at that later time.

The Reeve will now repay the Miller for his telling of how the soberer carpenter aspect of his personality has been outdone by the sexually reckless Nicholas disposition: 'This dronke Millere hath ytoold us heer / How that bigyled was a carpenter, / Peraventure in scorn, for I am oon. / And by youre leve, I shal hym quite anoon; / Right in his cherles termes wol I speke.' (*Pro RvT* 3913-15)

The Reeve's Tale

King Richard's tyrannical disposition is alluded to in the following description of this tale's miller: 'Pipen he koude and fisshe, and nettes beete, / And turn coppes, and wel wrastle and sheete.' (*RvT* 3927-28) 'Pipen he koude,' establishes an immediate connection between this tale's miller and the *GP's* drunken Miller: 'A baggepipe wel koude he blowe and sowne.' (*GP* 565) Probably 'fisshe, and nettes beete' is best explained when taken with the following lines: 'And drinken good wyn precious, / And preche us poverte and distresse, / And fisshen hemsilf great richesse / With wily nettis that they caste.'[93] This 'turn coppes' description suggests the lifting of glasses in a drinking session; 'Wel wrastle and sheete' implying that the dangerous reality behind this tale's miller has the ability and the inclination to overcome and 'sheete / shroud' those that attempt to oppose his increasingly tyrannical demands.

The tale's 'yonge povre scolers two' (*RvT* 4002) reside at 'A greet college / Men clepen the Soler Halle at Cantebregge;' (*RvT* 3989-90) known as the King's Hall, this Latin word *sol* / sun presents a powerful symbol of royalty. To further assist us in our identification of these hidden figures the

---

[93] Riverside, p. 751. *The Romance of the Rose*, pp. 6180-83.

'crowned' presence of the King Richard is hinted in both the young scholar Aleyn and the tale's miller swearing with the identical and significant oath: 'Thanne wil I be bynethe, by my croun;' (*RvT* 4041) 'They gete hym nat so lightly, by my croun.' (*RvT* 4099)

This miller's wife is described to be 'ycomen of noble kyn; / The 'person' of the toun hir fader was.' (*RvT* 3942-43) Surely this insertion of the word 'person' signifies far more than the present regarding of her being the 'illegitimate daughter of a parson, who had consequently paid her dowry.' (Riverside, p. 850) Far more likely that Queen Isabel's hidden nobility is being indicated here by means of her father being the 'person' of France's law and its body politic: its *persona publica*. The granting of 'ful many a panne of bras' (*RvT* 3944) with his daughter's hand in marriage to the reality behind this tale's miller alludes to Charles VI's substantial marriage portion of eight hundred thousand francs of gold; the recorded sum of Isabel's dowry paid to King Richard on their marriage.

The wife's pride in the social status of her kin, and of her upbringing in a nunnery, recalls the *GP*'s figure of the Prioress figure that 'Peyned hire to countrefete cheere / Of court, and to been estalich of manere, / And to ben holden digne of reverence.'(*GP* 139-41) The tale's most interesting compound word comes in the following passage: 'And eek, for she was somdel smoterlich, / She was as digne as water in a dich, / And ful of hoker and of bisemare. / Hir thoughte that a lady sholde hire spare, / What for hire kyndrede and hir nortelrie, / That she hadde lerned in the nonnerie.' (*RvT* 3963-68) The present explanations of 'smoterlich: besmirched, sullied ('in reputation, by her illegitimacy;') are probably incorrect;[94] this problematic word suggests a figurative interpretation is required. I therefore take it to be the following compound: 'smo / ter / lich;' smo / small (Scottish 'sma;') *ter* is the root of the Latin word *tertius* / one third, the tercelet being so-named because the male bird is commonly a third less in body size than the female; 'lich' or 'lic' being an earlier English word for body. A lich-gate being a 'body-gate;' the churchyard gate with a porch, under which a coffin could at that time be rested while the introductory portion of the burial service was being held at the church. The term 'lichewake' conveyed 'the watch or wake held over the body of the dead overnight;' (OE licham = body + waecc = watch).[95]

It follows that what appears to be suggested by this word 'smoterlich' is that her being a young child, the reality behind this wife has a body size

---

[94] Ibid. p. 79.
[95] Coredon, Christopher p. 177.

that's approximately one-third less in proportion to that of the average wife. Possibly because of the smallness of her stature she feels her own inferiority amongst the other females at the royal court, and therefore requests from others a display of the high opinion that she believes should be given to her due to 'hire kyndrede and hir nortelrie.'

The Cook's Prologue

The ongoing allegorical theme suggests that the *Cook's Prologue and Tale* covers the final period of the ongoing history. In the late *Manciple's Prologue* we find that this drunken Cook has yet to tell his tale: 'This Cook, that was ful pale and no thyng reed, / Seyde to our Host, "So God my soule blesse, / As ther is falle on me swich hevynesse, / Noot I nat why, that me were levere slepe / Than the beste gallon wyn in Chepe." / "Wel," quod the Maunciple, "If it may doon ese / To thee, sire Cook, and to no wight displese, / Which that here rideth in this compaignye, / And that oure Hoost wole, of his curteisye, / I wol as now excuse thee of thy tale."' (*Pro MancT* 20-29)

The desperate social conditions of those final years of the reign are implied in the Host's words to the Cook: 'Now telle on, Roger; looke that it be good, / For many a pastee hastow laten blood, / And many a Jakke of Dovere hastow sold / That hath

147

been twies hoot and twies coold. / Of many a pilgrym hastow Cristes curs, / For of thy percely yet they fare the wors, / That they han eten with thy stubbel goos, / For in thy shoppe is many a flye loos.'(*Pro MancT* 4345-52) 'Many a pastee' could be a pun on 'past years;' those in which the reality behind this Cook had caused the murder and impoverishment of his subjects. 'Jakke of Dovere' implies the hidden presence of the brutal John Holland, son of Joan of Kent, and therefore King Richard's half-brother. John Holland had twice committed 'hot' murderous outrages against Richard's subjects, and in a short space of time following each incident he had been returned 'cold' into the power afforded to him through his royal connections and privileges.

Probably John Holland is referred to here as 'Jakke of Dovere' because of the family's connection with Dover, the main Kentish town. Unless the above is an acceptable reading, in my opinion this 'Jack of Dover' term remains confusing and obscure: 'The meaning is not certain, but the expression is usually explained as a twice-cooked pie, i.e., one that is stale and has been warmed up. Skeat compares "Jack of Paris," used in this sense ... Robinson records a suggestion of Kittredge that the name (like "poor John," "John Dory") might have been applied to a fish ... For references to ordinances against bad food (pies "not befitting, and sometimes stinking,") see Bowden.' (*Riverside*, p. 853)

Obviously the above mention of 'many a pilgrym' implies King Richard's subjects; they certainly did 'fare the wors' on the 'percely' and 'stubbel goos' served to them by this cook. Apparently as far back as the Ancient Greeks, this word 'parsley' has carried association with death. Unlike the plumper 'green goose' that had been fed on the fruit of the corn; the 'stubbel goos' represented the more emancipated goose that had fed itself amongst the stubble chaff following the corn's removal. Here Chaucer could be implying that the above mentioned 'pilgrims' found it difficult to achieve a robust and healthy diet after the 'fruyt' of their labours in the fields had been removed to the tables of others less deserving than themselves; that is, taken to the boards of those that continuously feasted themselves on the 'green goose.'

The Cook's Tale

This Cook represents King Richard and the 'maister' figures his subjects. This tale's 'prentys' is described to be a 'revelour / That haunteth dys, riot, or paramour.'(*ClT* 4391-92 When that 'his maister hym bithoghte, / Upon a day, whan he his papir soghte, / Of a proverb that seith this same

149

word: / "Wel bet is roten appul out of hoord / Than that it rotie al the remenaunt." / So fareth it by a riotous servaunt; / It is ful lasse harm to lete hym pace, / Than he shende alle the servantz in the place. / Therfore his maister yaf hym acquitance,' / And bad hym go, with sorwe and with mischance!'(*ClT* 4403-4412) It seems to me this 'riotous servaunt' not having been given the necessary assistance when he his 'papir soghte' alludes to the king's inability to keep himself in power when Henry Bolingbroke returned to claim his lands, and later the crown.

In 1400 the above mentioned Jack of Dover / John Holland plotted an uprising that was intended to assassinate the newly crowned King Henry and his sons; following from this he and his supporters planned to return Richard to the throne. Apparently it was partly due to their betrayal by one of the members that the plot failed. From that time onwards Henry became fully aware of the threat that keeping Richard alive posed to his personal safety; and also to that of his family and his many supporters. John Holland was caught and beheaded on the 16th of January 1400. Shortly following this, on the 14th February of the same year, the former king was pronounced to have died in prison.

Introduction to the Man of Law's Tale

The first thing we notice in this Introduction is that the Host's dates it to be 18th. April: 'He wiste it was the eightetethe day / Of Aprill, that is messager to May.'(MLT 5-6) Believing that these tales are primarily an attempt to convey an allegorical description of King Richard's reign, my reading of this April 18th commencement suggests a significant allusion to Easter Day; but to the year 1378; rather than the 1387 dating taht has sbeen suggested by others. Although he was enthroned on 16th of July in 1377, Richard's first Easter Day as king was on April 18[th.] 1378.

This tale's 'Introduction to the Man of Law's Tale' is extremely informative and can be best understood within the context of it being a humourous response to the comments on Chaucer's 'lewed' attempts to rhyme 'in swich Englissh as he kan.' (*MLT* 49) Chaucer the Narrator will here counter the Man of Law's complaint of his ignorance by putting the following examples of 'lewedness' into the mouth of a person whose own literary inaccuracies are shown to be numerous. An ignorance that's even declared to be unaware of the difference between prose and rime royal: 'Several puzzling problems are raised by the *Introduction*. It contains a list of the heroines celebrated in the *Legend of Good Women*. But eight of the women named are not actually treated in the *Legend* and two whose story is there told (Cleopatra and Philomela) are not mentioned by the Man of Law ... The Man of Law's declaration '*I speke in prose*' probably indicates that the *Introduction* was not written to precede the *Tale of Constance,* both prologue and his tale being in rime royal! ... Possibly the idea that the children were hanged was derived by Chaucer from Jean de Meun's statement that Medea strangled them ... No such incident is mentioned in the *Legend of Medea* (*LGW,* 1580ff.) ... Alceste, Alcestis. Her story is not in the *Heroides* ... *Metamorphosios,* genitive (Metamorphoseos), dependent upon Liber, Libri, in the full title. Strictly speaking, the form should be *Metamorphoseon.*'[96]

The royal extravagances and debts are often mentioned in the historical records. Be it a king or a member of the impoverished peasantry, in time poverty may lead a person into the sin of blaming Christ for having provided another with greater wealth than oneself, and this in turn could result in another becoming the object of envious and malicious anger. In the final years of the reign, his being so heavily in debt was undoubtedly an important factor when King Richard's tyrannical rule in that period is fully considered; that is, those financial liabilities that led up to his expropriation

---

[96]Robinson, Complete Works, pp.690-691.

of the estates of his more affluent subjects, especially those belonging to the former appellant lords that had previously restrained his financial excesses. For reasons that I will detail later in this book, I believe it's the spirit of the murdered Duke of Gloucester that's implied to be speaking the following: 'My gold caused my mordre, sooth to sayn.'(*NPT* 3021)

The following lines are therefore relevant indicators of King Richard's reign during those final years: 'Maugree thyn heed, thou most for indigence / Or stele, or begge, or borwe thy despence! / Thow blamest Crist and seist ful bitterly / He mysdeparteth richesse temporal; / Thy neighebor thou wytest sinfully, / And seist thou has to lite and he hath al. / "Parfay," seistow, "somtyme he rekene shal, / Whan that his tayl shal brennen in the gleede, / For he noght helpeth needfulle in hir neede." / Herkne what is the sentence of the wise: / "Bet is to dyen than have indigence; / Thy selve neighebor wol thee despise." / If thou be povre, farwel thy reverence! / Yet of the wise man take this sentence: / "Alle the dayes of povre men been wikke." / Be war, thefore, er thou come to that prikke!'(*Pro MLT* 104-119)

In order to impress on King Richard his essential need to remain financially secure a comparison is drawn between the wise example of the noble and prudent people who prosper through foreign trade and the foolishness of those others that attempt to thrive by reckless speculation: 'O riche marchauntz, ful of wele been yee, / O noble, o prudent folk, as in this cas! / Youre bagges been nat fild with ambes as, / But with sys cynk, that renneth for your chaunce; / At Cristemasse myrie may ye daunce! / Ye seken lond and see for yowre wynnynges; / As wise folk ye knowen al th'estaat / Of regnes; ye been fadres of tidynges / And tales, bothe of pees and of debaat.' (*MLT* 122-130)

The Man of Law's Tale

Considered with the rest of Chaucer's compositions this tale's figure of Constance implies Queen Anne's presence. Chaucer's praises of the young queen are often found within his various works: 'I prey to God in honour hire susteene, / And wolde she were of al Europe the queene.' (*MLT* 160-61) The tale's male figures imply contrasting good and evil dispositions within King Richard. Possibly, the figures of the Sowdanesse: a 'root of iniquitee;' (*MLT* 358) and Donegild that 'traitour was to hire ligeance,' (*MLT* 895) imply the hidden presence of Joan of Kent, King Richard's disreputable mother. Chaucer's disapproval of what he may have known to be Joan's bad influence on her son may well be implied in the 'auctor / author' gloss that's placed directly opposite the above 'root of iniquitee' description in the margin of the early Hengwrt manuscript.

In order to corrupt their sons these two mothers resort to the stratagem of gluttony: 'Heere may men feeste and roialtee biholde, / And deyntees mo than I kan yow devyse; / But al to deere they boghte it er they ryse.' (*MLT* 418-20) 'The Sowdan and the Cristen everichone / Been al tohewe and stiked at the bord.' (*MLT* 429-30) The Pardoner pilgrim is certainly aware of the connection that exists between gluttony and unprincipled behaviour: 'O glotonye, on thee wel oghte us pleyne! / O, wiste a man how manye maldyes / Folwen of excesse and of glotonyes, / He wolde been the moore measurable / Of his diete, sittynge at his table.' (*PardT* 512 -16)

The Man of Law's blaming of Constance's maltreatment on her father's neglect of not having consulted a more favourable horoscope before her departure to 'Surrye' suggests King Richard's pathetic attempt to disregard the way he had mistreated Queen Anne: 'Crueel Mars hath slayn this mariage. / Infortunant ascendent tortuous, / Of which the lord is helplees falle, allas, / Out of his angle into the derkeste hous! / O Mars, o atazir, as in this cas! / O fieble moone, uhappy been thy paas! / Thou knyttest thee ther thou art nat received; / Ther thou were weel, fro thennes artow weyved. / Imprudent Emperour of Rome, allas! / Was ther no philosophre in al thy toun? / Is no tyme bet than oother in swich cas? / Of viage is ther noon eleccioun, / Namely to folk of heigh condicioun? / (*GP* 301-15) This astrological dating presented Chaucer with an excellent opportunity to insert a time sequence into his tale, one that corresponded with the beginning of Queen Anne's journey from Bohemia. That is, a planet ascends indirectly when in a tortuous sign, and those that climb most obliquely to the horizon are inclusively from Capricorn to Gemin, the prevailing planetary movement at the commencement of Anne's departure to England in December of 1381.

Introduction to the Squire's Tale

The *Squire's Tale* appears to be best suited to follow that told us by the Man of Law; and in the majority of manuscripts it's the one that does: 'Of the thirty-five MSS in which the *EpiMLT* appears, six read "Sommonour / Sompnour," twenty-eight "Squier,' and one (the late Selden) "Shipman."' (*Riverside*, p. 863) Certainly 'my joly body schal a tale telle,' (*MLT* 1185) suggests the courtly Squire's presence. Not only this we also find that the 'benigne curteisye' of the previous tale's 'Sowdan of Surrye' is echoed here in the 'benigne' qualities of this tale's King of Sarray; Constance's 'heigh beautee' being recalled in Canacee's beauty being 'so heigh a thing' that the Squire claims himself unable to adequately describe its excellence.

The Squire's Tale

As in the previous tale a gluttonous feast is prepared, a meal 'so solempne and so ryche / That in this world ne was ther noon it lyche.' (*SqT* 61-2) The 'strange knyght, that cam thus sodeynly' (*SqT* 89) 'after the thridde cours' (*SqT* 76) implies a contrasting disposition of King Richard to that personified in the previous tale's Sowdan of Surrye and this tale's noble King of Sarray.

Although this tale's knight is described to possess: 'So heigh reverence and obeisaunce, / As wel in speche as in contenaunce, / That Gawayn, with his olde curteisye, / Though he were comen ayeyn out of Fairye, / Ne koude hym nat amende with a word;' (*SqT* 93-97) when he is later described to be in the company 'of lusty Venus children deere,' (*SqT* 272) his behaviour implies him to be such a lecherous person. In order to impress us further in this matter his conduct is paralleled to that of the immoral Lancelot whose illicit liason with Queen Guinevere brought about the downfall of King Arthur's kingdom: 'Who koude telle yow the forme of daunces / So unkouthe, swiche fresshe contenaunces, / Swich subtil lookyng and dissymulynges / For drede of

157

jalouse mennes aperceyvynges? / No man but Launcelot, and he is deed.' (*SqT* 83-87) Set in an allegorical framework that describes Queen Anne as Canacee, and later as the falcon, this tale portrays the young queen's sudden awareness that the previously held belief of her husband's honesty in the claims of the truth of his love towards her had been mistaken.

The tale's theme of a love betrayal is ingeniously conveyed by means of the mirror and ring 'sent to my lady Canacee.' (*SqT* 144) The magical mirror has the quality of detecting a lover's treachery: 'If any lady bright / Hath set hire herte on any maner wight, / If he be fals, she shal his tresoun see.' (*SqT* 137–39) The mirror discloses such a 'betrayal' to Canacee, and its revelation disturbs her so much: 'In hire sleep, right for impressioun / Of hire mirour, she hadde a visioun' (*SqT* 371-72) that disturbs and places her on the path leading to the equally grieving falcon. Additional to what she has observed in the mirror, the ring's magical powers of communication enables her to comprehend the language of all the 'fowel that fleeth under the hevene / That she ne shal wel understonde his stevene, / And knowe his menyng openly and pleyn.' (*SqT* 149-51) With the miraculous properties possessed by the 'mirror' and the 'ring' the Squire is provided with the means for the telling of his tale, and is therafter able to progress towards the 'sentence' of his narrative: 'The knotte why that every tale be toold.' (*SqT* 401)

The falcon's anguish on the realisation of its betrayal being expressed in comparable terms to the appearance and behaviour of the tale's strange knight: 'Right so this god of loves ypocryte / Dooth so his cerymonyes and obeisaunces, / And kepeth in semblaunt alle his observaunces / That sownen into gentillesse of love. / As in a toumbe is al the faire above, / And under is the corps, swich as ye woot, / Swich was this ypocrite, bothe coold and hoot. / And in this wise he served his entente / That, save he feend, noon wiste what he mente.' (*SqT* 514-522)

In the sorrowful expressions of the tale's falcon; Queen Anne's figured grief on realising her husband's falseness is surely to be considered as being one of the most moving and heart-felt telling of a misguided love to be found in the whole of English literature. Not even the passage of six centuries and more dimishes the distress felt by Chaucer's description of this young queen's anguish: 'Al innocent of his crouned malice, / Forfered of his deeth, as thoughte me, / Upon his othes and his seuretee, / Graunted hym love, upon this condicioun, / That everemoore myn honour and renoun / Were saved, bothe privee and apert; / This is to seyn, that after his desert, / I yaf hym al myn herte and al my thought - / God woot and he, that ootherwise noght - / And took his herte in chaunge of myn for ay. / But sooth is seyd, goon sithen many a day, / A trewe wight and a theef thenken nat oon.' (*SqT* 526-37)

The Franklin's Tale

The connection to be drawn between this Franklin and the previous tale's Squire are found in the earlier denial of his rhetorical abilities being repeated by the Franklin: 'It moste been a rethor excellent / That koude his colours longynge for that art, / If he sholde hire discryven every part. / I am noon swich, I moot speke as I kan;' (*SqT* 38-41) 'Have me excused of my rude speche. / I lerned nevere rethorik, certeyn; / Thyng that I speke, it moot be bare and pleyn.' (*FranT* 718-20). Although the tale's location has now been changed from the land of the Tartars to that of the Bretons, it implies a continuation of the previous narrative of separated lovers: 'Thus lete I Canacee hir hauk kepyng; / I wol namoore as now speke of hir ryng / Til it come eft to purpose for to seyn / How that this faucon gat hire love ageyn / Repentant, as the storie telleth us, / By mediacion of Cambalus, / The kynges sone, of which I yow tolde.' (*SqT* 651-657) With this 'kynges sone' phrase Chaucer is probably alluding to an opposite, a more honourable disposition within King Richard's personality.

Approximately two months pass between the start and the close of the *Squire's Tale*: from 'the laste Idus of March' (*SqT* 47) to early May when 'Appollo whirleth up his chaar so hye / Til that the god Mercurius hous, the slye.' (*SqT* 671-72) In the absence of her husband Arveragus: 'On the sixte morwe of May;' (*FranT* 906) a 'lusty squier, servant to Venus, / Which that ycleped was Aurelius,' (*FranT* 937-38) declares his love for Dorigen, and by means of a sly illusion attempts to gain her compliance with his sexual desires.

In the previous tale we had learned that the tercelet and falcon had separated 'for his honour, as ofte it happeth so;' (*SqT* 592) likewise, Arveragus and Dorigen were parted when he set out 'to seke in armes worshipe and honour.' (*FranT* 811) In both tales, prior to their separation the happiness of the lovers is described to have been of a short duration: 'lenger than a yeer or two;' (*SqT* 574) 'a yeer and moore.' (*FranT* 806) The intensity of the falcon's despair over the loss of her love: 'Tho shrighte this faucon yet moore pitously / Than ever she dide,' (*SqT* 472-473) is repeated here in this tale's description of Dorigen's grief over her loss of Arveragus: 'For his absence wepeth she and siketh, / As doon thise noble wyves whan hem liketh. / She moorneth, waketh, wayleth, fasteth, pleyneth.' (*FranT* 817-819)

When its allegory has been understood the supreme good the tale conveys is immediately seen to be a wife's right, especially so when she has previously been given that choice, to refuse the sexual advances of a philandering husband. At the tale's commencement Arveragus had promised Dorigen greater freedom than 'swich lordshipe as men han over hir wyves;' (*FranT* 742) in the initial tenderness of his love towards her he had promised that their future relationship would never result in his imposition of a husband's right to sexual mastery: 'Of his free wyl he swoor hire as a knyght / That nevere in al his lyf he, day ne nyght, / Ne sholde upon hym take no maistrie / Agayn hir wyl, ne kithe hire jalousie, / But hire obeye, and folwe hir wyl in al, / As any lovere to his lady shal.' (*FranT* 745-50)

If solely to be taken as being her response to a dangerous coastline, to a natural obstruction in God's creation that prevent her husband's return, Dorigen's lament over 'the grisly rokkes blake' (*FranT* 859) is immediatelty seen to be too melodramatic. However, when these same 'rocks' are read as being moral impediments in the one previously loved for his believed opposite qualities of 'heigh reverence and obeisaunce;' her grief over the event becomes the more acceptable: 'But wolde God that alle thise rokkes blake / Were sonken into helle for his sake!' (*FranT* 891-92) Notice this description of 'rokkes blake / Were sonken into helle for his sake!' Such a figurative reading of 'rocks' is to be found in those biblical verses that indicate a sinful nature unable of being penetrated by the living seed of Christian morality:

> A sower went out to sow his seed: and as he sowed, some fell by the way side; and it was trodded down, and the fowls of the air devoured it. (Luke 8, verse 6).

> And some fell upon a rock; and as soon as it was sprung up, it withered away, because it lacked moisture. (Luke, 8, verse 13).

When we have become aware of the tale's deeper allegorical level its tale's theme is not difficult to comprehend. Deeply hurt by her husband's Aurelius-like behaviour: that of a 'lusty squire, servant to Venus,' (*FranT* 937) and until King Richard provides her with evidence of his having returned to his former Averagus aspect: 'that was hir housbonde and hir love also,' (*FranT* 922) Queen Anne will insist on the protection provided by his earlier pledge of being her 'servant in love.' (*FranT* 793) This is the only way that I can make any sense of her promise to grant her love to the Aurelius disposition: 'Whan ye han maad the coost

so clene / Of rokkes that ther nys no stoon ysene.'
(*FranT* 995-96)

The garden description at the tale's ending: 'Nevere was ther gardyn of swich prys / But if it were the verray paradys;' (*FranT* 911-12) suggests the traditional *paradis d'amour* of unbridled sexual passions. Only after becoming aware of the tale's division of King Richard's psyche between the contrasting figures of Arveragus and Aurelius; dispositions in which each aspect retains a certain degree of its opposite, can we make sense of Arveragus's insistence that Dorigen keep her oath to Aurelius, and that she thereafter remain silent on the matter: 'I yow forbade, up peyne of deeth, / That nevere, whil thee lasteth lyf ne breeth, / To no wight telle thou of this aventure.' (*FranT* 1480-83)

This tale's main moral goodness appears when Aurelius finds himself unable to compel Dorigen to keep her promise of a pledge that he knows to have been fraudulently gained by means of a 'sly' illusion regarding the 'seeming' removal of the allegorical rocks. From this time onwards in the tale we conclude that King Richard seeks to retain what is left of Queen Anne's respect towards him, and because of this he will keep himself true to the Franklin's words of love's disappearance when it's obtained through a fraudulent and enforced sexual mastery: 'Love wol nat been constreyned by maistrye. / When maistrie comth, the God of Love anon / Beteth his wynges, and farewel, he is gon!' (*FranT* 764-66) Instead of his initial sexual intention within the 'garden,' Aurelius prefers 'to suffer wo / Than I departe the love bitwix yow two.' (*FranT* 1531-32) The Aurelius disposition of King Richard is incapable of acting contrary to the earlier Arveragus promise of granting his wife the right of sexual refusal: 'My trouthe I plighte, I shal yow never repreve / Of no biheste, and heere I take my leve, / As of the trewest and the best wyf / That evere yet I knew in al my lyf.' (*FranT* 1537-154)

Although King Richard may have provided Queen Anne with 'illusionary' evidence of his having removed from his court the one; perhaps the many, with whom his behaviour had caused her such emotional anguish; nevertheless, he seems to have taken his earlier promise and her present words to heart: 'Lat swiche folies out of youre herte slide. / What deyntee sholde a man han in his lyf / For to go love another mannes wyf, / That hath hir body whan so that hym liketh?' (*FranT* 1002-05)

The tale implies Queen Anne's awareness that her husband's removal of the 'rocks' was nothing other than a deception symptomatic of one connected with 'Mercurius hous, the slye;' that highly relevant description that closed the previous tale. The deviousness of one that creates such a 'sly' illusion as was figured in this tale: 'And whan this maister that this magyk wroughte / Saugh it was tyme, he clapte his handes two, / And farewel! Al oure revel was ago. / And yet remoeved they nevere out of the hous. / Whil they saugh al this sighte merveillous.' (*FranT* 1202-06)

The Physician's Tale

To underline and thereby consolidate our awareness of the previous tale's significant moral, the Physician replaces the opposites of Arveragus and Aurelius with the more extreme figures of Virginius and Apius. The evil of the former tale's attempt of sexual entrapment is now shown to be divested of all pretence that such behaviour could have been inspired by *caritas* love.

Unlike Arveragus' pathetic attempt to persuade Dorigen into commiting the sexual act against her wishes: 'Truthe is the hyeste thing that man may kepe;' (*FrankT* 1479) this tale's figure of Virginius prefers the choice of his daughter's death rather than her defilement by the animalistic Apius (ape) disposition. In both of these tales the villainous objective is the attempted sexual violation of a betrayed female. In real terms the previous tale's 'sly illusion' of the removed rocks is no different to the equally sly and evil intentions of this tale's figure of Apius: 'Anon the feend into his herte ran, / And taughte hym sodeynly that he by

slyghte / The mayden to his purpos wynne myghte.'
(*PhyT* 130-32)

The Physician's descriptions of Virginia's physical beauty and her virtuous behaviour implies Chaucer's recognition of such qualities being present in the fourteen-year-old Queen Anne on her arrival in England:

> This mayde of age twelve yeer was and tweye,
> In which that Nature hadde swich delit,
> For right as she kan peynte a lilie whit,
> And reed a rose, right with swich peynture
> She peynted hath this noble creature,
> Er she were born, upon hir lymes fre,
> Where as by right swiche colours sholde be;
> And Phebus dyed hath hire tresses grete
> Lyk to the stremes of his burned heete.
> And if that excellent was hire beautee,
> A thousand foold moore virtuous was she.
> (*PhyT* 30-40)

The shameful insistence of Arveragus that Dorigen must accompany Aurelius into the garden, and his demand of her silence regarding such a forced compliance, is recalled here in the Physician's assertion that sin can neither be hidden from God nor ignored by a man's own conscience: 'The worm of conscience may agryse / Of wikked lyf, though it so pryvee be / That no man woot therof but God and he.' (*PhyT* 280-82)

Probably the Physician's censuring of those that fail to protect their wards by their allowing them to riot 'at feestes, revels, and at daunces / That been occasions of daliaunces,' (*PhyT* 65-66) is to be taken as a warning to those French governesses charged with overseeing the young Queen Isabel's behaviour: 'And ye maistresses, in youre olde lyf, / That lords doghtres han in governaunce, / Ne taketh of my wordes no displesaunce. / Thenketh that ye been set in governynges / Of lords doghtres oonly for two thynges: / Outher for ye han kept youre honestee, / Or ells ye han falle in freletee, / And knowen wel ynough the olde daunce, / And han forsaken fully swich meschaunce / And evermo; therefore, for Cristes sake, / To teche hem vertu looke that ye ne slake.' (*PhyT* 72-82) This censure being expressed with the deepest of feelings: 'And taketh kep of that that I shal seyn: / Of alle tresons sovereyn pestilence / Is whan a wight bitrayseth innocence.' (*PhyT* 90-92)

When considering such an allegorical reading of the tale it's surely significant that immediately before his final voyage to Ireland in 1399, King Richard had replaced Queen Isabel's governesses on the pretext that they were imprudent and wasteful. Being that extravagance had not previously appeared to be a significant issue with this king; in my opinion it's far more likely that his fear was their indiscretion when in charge of his young wife while he was absent from the country that caused of his main concern. It's more than likely therefore that the above concern should not be read in the following manner: 'This digression on the responsibilities of parents and guardians has often been regarded as unduly obtrusive, and historical explanations have been sought ... there is no necessity to seek an actual event behind sentiments that are ... conventional, however awkwardly introduced.' (*Riverside*, p. 903)

The Introduction to the Pardoner's Tale

Initially the Host appears to be emotionally disturbed by the above tale: 'Oure Hooste gan to swere as he were wood; / "Harrow!" quod he, "by nayles and by blood! / This was a fals cherl and a fals justice. / As shameful deeth as herte may devyse / Come to thise juges and hire advocatz."' (*Pard Intro* 287-291) On reflection however he appears to blame Virginia's death on her gifts of Fortune and of Nature rather than the villainy of others: 'Algate this sely mayde is slayn, allas! / Allas, to deere bought she beautee! / Wherfore I seye al day that men may see / That yiftes of Fortune and of Nature / Been cause of deeth to many a creature. / Hire beautee was hire deth, I dar

169

wel sayn. / Allas, so pitously as she was slayn! / Of bothe yiftes that I speke of now / Men han ful ofte moore for harm than prow. / But trewely, myn owene maister deere, / This is a pitous tale for to heere. / But nathelees, passé over; is no fors.'(*Intro PardT* 292-303)

The transfer of dispositions from the Host to the Pardoner seems here to be signalled by the close repetition of the Host's 'by Seint Ronyan!' into the Pardoner's 'by Seint Ronyon;' this having been a difficult saint to determine his identity: 'Taken by Skeat as a reference to a St. Ronan ... Haskell argues for the appropriateness of this saint to a Celt venerated in Brittany ... However the name may be a popular variant pronounciation of "Ninan," a Scottish saint widely known in the fourteenth century.' (*Riverside* p. 904) I read it differently, that this Ronyan / Ronyon is a punning on 'ronyon / ronion:' (Fr. *Rogne* = scab, mange; that is a mangy scurvy person. Shakespeare has: 'Out of my door, you witch, you polecat, you ronyon.' (*The Merry Wives of Windsor* Act 4, sc. 2)

Probably we need to recall that the Pardoner's travelling companion is the Summoner, a pilgrim who is able to readily transfer himself into the Pardoner, and is described to be such a scabby faced pilgrim: 'With scalled browes blake and piled berd. / Of his visage, children were aferd. / Ther nas quyk-silver, lytarge, ne brymstoon, / Boras, ceruce, ne oille of tarter noon, / Ne oynement that wolde clense and byte, / That hym myghte helpen of his whelks white, / Nor of the knobbes sittynge on his chekes.' (*GP* 627-633) The Pardoner is certainly aware of his travelling companion's condition, and therefore this seems to underline the significance of the saint's name: 'A lecherous thyng is wyn, and dronkenesse / Is ful of stryvyng and of wrecchednesse. / O dronke man, disfigured is thy face.'(*PardT* 549-51)

The Pardoner's Prologue

The *Pardoner's Prologue* presents us with ample evidence of this pilgrim's covetousness: 'I preche of no thyng but for coveityse, / Therfore my theme is yet, and evere was, *Radix malorium est Cupiditas* / Thus kan I preche again that same vice / Which that I use, and this is avarice.' (Pard.Pro. 425-28) Chaucer does not hold back from detailing this pilgrim's lack of human pity, or of the reasons for his love of money: 'I wol noon of the apostles countreferte / I wol have moneie, wolle, chese, and whete, / Al were it yeven of the povereste page, / Or of the povereste wydwe in a village, / Al sholde hir children sterve for famine. Nay, I wol drynke licour of the vayne / And have a joly wenche in every toun.' (*Pard Prol*. 447-53)

Probably it's the Host's awareness of the financial difficulties that he now confronts due to this Pardoner's 'joly wenche' routine that brings about his angry response to the Pardoner's request of money: 'I wolde I hadde thy coillons in myn hond / In stide of relikes or of seintuarie. / Lat kutte hem of, I wol thee helpe hem carie; / They shul be shryned in an hogges toord!' (*PardT* 941-55)

The Pardoner's Tale

The Pardoner is aware of the dangers that accompany the condition of 'wyn and dronkenesse;' (*PardT* 484) and he illustrates this in the following examples: 'Lo, how that drunken Looth, unkyndely, / Lay by his daughters two, unwityngly; / So dronke he was, he nyste what he wroghte. / Herodes, whoso wel the stories soghte, / Whan he of wyn was replete at his feeste, / Right at his owene table he yaf his heeste / To sleen the Baptist John, ful giltelees. / Senec seith a good word doutelees; / He seith he kan no difference fynde / Bitwix a man that is out of his mynde / And a man which that is dronkelewe, / But that woodnesse, yfallen in a shrewe, / Perservereth lenger than doth dronkenesse.' (*PardT* 485-497)

Other moral failings condemned in this tale are gluttony; gambling, and 'great' and 'false' swearing: 'Allas, the shorte throte, the tender mouth, / Maketh that est and west and north and south, / In erthe, in eir, in water, men to swynke / To gete a gloutoun deyntee mete and drynke!' (*PardT* 517-520) The tale's extended condemnation of gambling implies King Richard's involvement in such a dangerous habit: 'If that a prynce useth hasardrye, / In alle governaunce and policye / He is, as by commune opinioun, / Yholde the lasse in reputacioun.' (*PardT* 599-602) 'Stilboun, that was a wys embassadour,' (*PardT* 603) would not destroy his reputation by forming an alliance with those that gambled: 'Sendeth othere wise embassadours; / For, by my trouthe, me were levere dye / Than I yow sholde to hasardours allye.' (*PardT* 614-616) The King of Parthia is described to have scorned King Demetrius by sending him a pair of gold dice: 'For he hadde used hasard ther-biforn; / For which he heeld his glorie or his renoun / At no value or reputacioun; / Lordes may fynden oother maner pley / Honest ynough to dryve the day awey.' (*PardT* 624-28)

This tale emphasises the difference that's to be found between 'great' and 'false' swearing: 'Gret sweryng is a thyng abhominable, / And fals sweryng is yet moore reprievable.' (*PardT* 631-32) Great swearing being such irreverences as: 'By Goddes precious herte ... By his nayles;' (*PardT* 651) false swearing being the disregarding of oaths previously affirmed with great solemnity: 'Of

173

sweryng seith the hooly Jeremye, / "Thou shalt swere sooth thyne othes, and nat lye, / And swere in doom and eek in rightwisnesse.'" (*PardT* 635-37) King Richard had sworn many oaths to his subjects, and eventually it was his continual breaking of these that resulted in their inability to accept his word in matters essential to them and to the future security of their families. Very few could eventually have trusted the reliability of his sworn promises, even when these were granted with 'great solemnity.' The most nortorious and therefore the final of these being his disregarding of his earlier promise to Henry Bolingbroke, that on his father's death he would be allowed to maintain his father's inheritance. It was the direct consequence of his breaking of this oath sworn 'in doom and eek in rightwisenesse' that brought about the downfall of his reign.

This tale's 'compaignye / Of yonge folk that hautenden folye,' (*PardT* 463-64) are surely to be taken as identical riotous and money-grasping presentations of King Richard: 'We thre been al ones.' (*PardT* 696) Here the tale's instructive moral of '*Radix malorum est Cupiditas,*' (*PardT* 426) not only signifies that love of money indicates spiritual death; also, that it can lead to physical death. Such deaths as are indicated within the tale when the 'oold man' points to the consequence that may befall those who pursue gold down the 'croked wey:' '"Now, sires," quod he, "if that yow be so leef / To fynde Deeth, turne up this croked wey, / For in that grove I lafte hym, by my fey, / Under a tree, and there he wole abyde; / Noght for your boost he wole him no thyng hyde. Se ye that ook? Right there ye shal hym fynde. / God save yow, that boghte again mankynde, / And yow amende! (*PardT.* 760-767)

The Clerk's Prologue

Regardless of Harry Bailly's request: 'Telle us som murie thing of aventures. / Youre termes, youre colours and youre figures, / Keepe hem in stoor til so be ye endite / Heigh style, as whan that men to kynges write / Speketh so pleyn at this tyme, we yow preye, / That we may understonde what ye seye;' (*ProClT* 15-20) the *Clerk's Tale* is composed in the 'heigh style, as whan that men to kynges write.' (*Pro ClT* 18) Furthermore, although the Host also demands that the Clerk should turn away from the temptation to 'Make us for oure olde synnes wepe,' (*ProClT* 13) he is informed that this request will only be be granted 'as fer as reson axeth.' (*ProClT* 25)

It would have been appropriate, shortly following his second marriage, to remind King Richard of his marital 'olde synnes' against such a praiseworthy first wife as Queen Anne: 'I seye that yvele it sit / To assaye a wyf whan that it is no nede, / And putten hire in angwyssh and in drede.' (*ClT* 459-462) Those in authority should not presume that Griselda's long-suffering submissiveness to her lord's hurtful ways will be echoed in the responses of their own mistreated subjects: 'O stormy peple! Unsad and evere untrewe! / Ay undiscreet and chaungynge as a fane! / Delitynge evere in rumbul that is newe, / For lyk the moone ay wexe ye and wane! / Ay ful of clappyng, deere ynogh a jane! / Youre doom is fals, youre constance yvele preveth; / A ful greet fool is he that on yow leeveth.' (*ClT* 995-1001)

Finding conclusive evidence of Chaucer having met Petrarch and having listened to the next tale in his company could be an interesting historical investigation for a future reader to consider. My allegorical reading of this prologue, and with it the depth of feelings described therein, suggests that such a meeting took place: 'The records indicate nothing as to the itinerary Chaucer followed in going to Italy and returning ... Studies of the time required for such journeys in the Middle Ages indicate that Chaucer may have had about 100 days in Italy out of the 174 spent on the journey ... Interesting speculations arise as to what literary associations Chaucer may have made on this, usually regarded as his first Italian journey. The questions which have most often been discussed are the possibility of a meeting between Chaucer and Petrarch at this time, either at Arqua or at Padua ... It is more likely that Chaucer was chosen for this mission because he knew Italian already than that he first became acquainted with Italian on this journey.' (*Life Records*, p. 40)

I consider that this tale's meeting between these two is described with such feeling that it seems highly improbable to have been fictitious. Why would Chaucer have fabricated such a momentous event in his life when the truth or otherwise of it would have been readily known to his contemporaries? Lack of 'definite' historical proof does not deter me in my acceptance that such an encounter took place. We need only to consider the deep and pronounced reverence with which the Clerk treats his details of the event: 'I wol yow telle a tale which that I / Lerned at Padowe of a worthy clerk, / As preved by his wordes and his werk. / He is now deed and nayled in his cheste; / I prey to God so yeve his soule reste! / Fraunceys Petrak, the lauriat poete, / Highte this clerk, whos rethorike sweete / Enlumyned al Ytaille of poetrie, / As Lynyan dide of philosophie, / Or lawe, or oother art particular; / But Deeth, that wol nat suffer us dwellen heer, / But as it were a twynklyng of an ye, / Hem bothe hath slay, and alle shul we dye.' (*ClT* 26-38)

Petrarch is within this short prologue twice praised as having been a 'worthy' man; and the Clerk presents us with a detailed and memorable description of what appears to have been an inspiring visit that he spent in the company of the 'lauriat poete' that Chaucer so greatly admired: 'But forth to tellen of this worthy man / That taughte me this tale, as I bigan, / I seye that first with heigh stile he enditeth, / Er he the body of his tale writeth, / A prohemye, in the which discryveth he / Pemond and of Saluces the contree, / And speketh of Apennyn, the hills hye, / That been the boundes of West Lumbardye, / And of Mount Vesulus in special, / Where as the Poo out of a welle small / Taketh his firste spryngyng and his sours, / That estward ay encresseth in his cours / To Emele-ward, to Ferrare, and Venyse, / The which along thyng were to devyse. / And trewely, as to my juggement, / Me thynketh it a thyng impertinent, / Save that he wole conveyne his mateere; / But this his tale, which that ye may heere.' (ClT 26-56)

I have been surprised that others question the authenticity of their meeting. That they fail to feel the thrill behind Chaucer's descriptions of his having met one that he so greatly esteemed. If not to convince his readers that the encounter was a real event, why would he have been so thorough in the descriptive detail of such a delightful venue, and with this shown his appreciation of having met

Petrarch. This belief is greatly strengthened at the tale's close when, in its *Lenvoy de Chaucer*, he identifies himself as being the Clerk of this tale.

The Clerk's Tale

King Richard is probably hinted in Walter's 'lust present ... / As for to hauke and hunte on every side / Wel ny alle othere cures leet he slyde;' (*ClT* 80-82) Queen Anne appears to be implied in the tale's portrayal of Griselda: 'As she an emperoures doghter were;' (*ClT* 168) and in the Clerk's comparison of God's favour of her grace as being the gift of one 'norissed in an emperoures halle.' (*ClT* 399) Griselda's efforts in establishing the common good is constantly stressed: 'The commune profit koude she redresse. / Ther nas discord, rancour, ne heavynesse / In al that land that she ne koude nat apese, / And wisely brynge hem alle in reste and ese.' (*ClT* 431-34) Most definitely, this description held its historical counterpart in Queen Anne's capable and consistent role as a virtuous and successful peacemaker; in her corrections of King Richard's tyrannical disregard of the necessary *caritas* love he should have displayed towards his subjects.

Although being ready to harshly criticise his sovereign's reckless behaviour; nevertheless, Chaucer does not seem to believe that a subject is justified to be in open revolt against God's chosen ruler. The Clerk considers: 'Every wight, in his degree, / Sholde be constant in adversitee.' (*ClT* 1146-47) Such patience would have been the correct Christian instruction, especially in those times of political tensions: 'As was Grisilde; therfore Petrak writeth / This storie, which with heigh stile he enditeth. / For sith a womman was so pacient / Unto a mortal man, wel moore us oghte / Receyven al in gree that God us sent.' (*ClT* 1146-52)

The Wife of Bath stanza at the tale's close is interesting; being absent from a large group of the manuscripts it appears to have been a late inclusion. Probably it was written following Chaucer's growing awareness and increasing concern over Queen Isabel extravagances at the royal court. Whereas Queen Anne's actions had been conducted towards securing social justice; Queen Isabel's 'maistrie' was directed towards self-glorification: 'It were ful hard to fynde now-a-dayes / In al a toun Grisildis thre or two; / For if that they were put to swiche assayes, / The gold of hem hath now so bade alayes / With bras, that thogh the coyne be fair at ye, / It wolde rather breste a-two than plye. / For which heere, for the Wyves love of Bathe - / Whos lyf and al hire secte God mayntene / In heigh maistrie, and ells were it scathe.' (*ClT* 1164-75).

I believe that Chaucer's heartfelt sorrow over Queen Anne's early death is the reason for his identifying of the tale's Grisilede with her; and then the naming of himself rather than a nameless Clerk with the following sentiments:

Lenvoy de Chaucer

Grisilde is deed, and eek hire pacience,
And bothe atones buryed in Ytaille;
For which I crie in open audience.
No wedded man so hardy be t'assaille
His wyves pacience in trust to fynde
Grisildis, for in certein he shal faille.
(*ClT* 1177-82)

Notice that although he cautions 'noble wyves ful of heigh prudence' (*ClT* 1183) to ensure 'no clerk have cause or diligence / To write of yow a storie of swich mervaille / As of Grisildis pacient and kynde;' (*ClT* 1183-87) he also adds the important proviso that as did Griselda, on achieving the 'governaille' they also exercise it 'for commune profit.' (*ClT* 1194)

The Merchant's Prologue

The Merchant's opening response to the Clerk's final words that 'archewyves' should 'be ay of chiere as light as leef on lynde, / And lat hym care, and wepe, and wrynge, and waille,' (*ClT* 1211-12) establishes a direct connection with his own tale: '"Wepyng and waylyng, care and oother sorwe / I knowe ynogh, on even and a-morwe," Quod the Marchant.' (*ProMerT* 1213-15) Queen Isabel having now become the wife in question, the Merchant draws a 'Host-like' comparison between her behaviour and that of the previous tale's figure of Queen Anne: 'I have a wyf, the worste that may be; / For thogh the feend to hire ycoupled were, / She wolde hym overmacche, I dar wel swere. / What sholde I yow reherce in special / Hir hye malice? She is a shrewe at al. / Ther is a long and large difference / Bitwix Grisildis grete pacience / And of my wyf the passyng crueltee. / Were I unbounden, also moot I thee, / I wolde nevere eft comen in the snare.' (*ProMerT* 1218-27)

The Merchant's Tale

The Merchant's period of wedlock: 'Thise monthes two, and moore nat, pardee,' (*MerT* 1234) suggests it respresents how short a time passed between January's wedding and the tale's pear tree incident. Whereas the January of this tale implies the fuller background presence of King Richard; Placebo and Justinus suggest opposing dispositions within this same figure. Damyan: dam / yan =

182

damned one; being a 'damned' disposition within the mixture. His presence within the tale represents a sexually forceful aspect of mind that's determined to gain the child Queen Isabel / May's compliance with his sexual lust.

When choosing a wife it was 'bitwixe ernest and game' (*MerT* 1594) that January 'atte laste apoynted hym on oon, / And leet alle othere from his herte goon, / And chees hire of his owene auctoritee.' (*MerT* 1595-97) Probably this mention of 'game' alludes to King Richard having initially jested on finding the seven-year-old Isabel's profile amongst those of the young ladies he was to consider as being suitable marriage candidates. January was the month of Richard's birth, and probably the name May indicates Isabel's symbolic role within the tale: 'She was lyk the bright morwe of May.' (*MerT* 1748) As I have previously mentioned, I believe Shakespeare was aware of these allegories and it's therefore possible that this is why he presented us with an identical description of King Richard's child queen: 'She came adorned hither like sweete May'.[97]

The vivid details of January's thoughts as he considers his young bride on their wedding night greatly assists us in our understanding of the tale's allegory: 'But nathelees yet hadde he greet pitee /

---

[97]Shakespeare's <u>Richard the Second,</u> Act V, sc. i, l. 79.

That thilke nyght offenden hire moste he, / And thoughte, "Allas! O tendre creature, / Now wolde God ye myghte wel endure / Al my corage, it is so sharp and keeene! / I am agast ye shul it nat susteene."' (*MerT* 1755-61) That is, whereas the country's Canon Law allowed the Merchant to 'play' with his seven year old child bride: 'For we han leve to pleye us by the lawe,' (*MerT* 1841) by that same statute he was also entrusted to abstain from sexual intercourse with her before she had reached her years of puberty.

This sexual denial is a predicament that troubles the apprehensive January as the wedding night approaches: 'God forbede that I dide al my myght!' (*MerT* 1761) It also suggests to us the reason why he attempts to reassure himself and his wife that 'it is no fors how longe that we pleye.' (*MerT* 1835) His problem being that the Damyan disposition within his psyche lusts so much to obtain full sexual intercourse with his young bride that January considers the denial of 'al my myght' is an affront to her on their wedding night: 'He rubbeth hire aboute hir tendre face, / And seyde thus, "Allas! I moot trespace / To yow, my spouse, and yow greetly offende / Er tyme come that I wil doun descende."'(*MerT* 1827-30)

Had sexual penetration taken place this self-confessed rude man: 'Ladyes, I prey yow that ye be nat wrooth; / I kan nat glose, I am a rude man,'

(*MerT* 2350-51) would surely have delighted in describing the event with an excess of crudeness. He certainly would not have confined his comments to January's 'playing' with his wife. He certainly displays no lack of vulgarity in his later description of Damyan's behaviour in the pear tree: 'And sodeynly anon this Damyan / Gan pullen up the smok, and in he throng.' (*MerT* 2352-53)

Damyan's sexual climax allows the soberer Merchant disposition within Richard's personality to regain its ascendancy; thereafter the previously described to be 'blind' January immediately recovers his sight, and his anguished cry over what he now 'sees' to have taken place is expressed in terms of his need to withdraw his penis out of her body: 'And up he yaf a roryng and a cry, / As dooth the mooder whan the child shal dye; / "Out! Help! Allas! Harrow!" he gan to crye, / "O stronge lady stoore, what dostow?"' (*MerT* 2364-67) His comparison of what he now understands to have taken place as the dying of a mother's child complements what he observes to have happened; probably, it's intended to signify the 'death' / loss of the child Queen Isabel's virginity; figuratively expressed here as being the 'death' of her childhood innocence.

Not surprisingly this act of sexual passion is described to have taken place in a garden resplendent with the established literary tokens of

185

sensuality: 'So fair a gardyn woot I nowher noon. / For, out of doute, I verraily suppose / That he that wroot the *Romance of the Rose* / Ne koude of it the beautee wel devyse.' (*MerT* 2030-33) It's also meaningful that January blames May for her encouragement over what has taken place. Within such an allegorical environment the pear tree conveys sexual enticement, and the Merchant's description of May's urge to eat of the tree's fruit should not therefore be simply read as 'the appetites of pregnant women.' (*Riverside*, p. 889) Rather than this it represents the Merchant's attempt to blame the immoral act that has taken place on the lustful female appetite of January's wife: '"Now sire," quod she, "For aught that may bityde, / I moste han of the peres that I see, / Or I moot dye, so soore longeth me / To eten of the smale peres grene. / Help, for hir love that is of hevene queene! / I telle yow wel, a womman in my plit / May han to fruyt so greet an appetite / That she may dyen but she of it have."' (*MerT* 2328-37)

Not surprisingly, in the tale's epilogue we find the Host representative of King Richard readily agreeing with the Merchant that the responsibility for what has taken place in the pear tree should be blamed on the passions of those tempting females that trap their male partners into commiting such a sin: 'Lo, whiche sleightes and subtilitees / In wommen been! For ay as bisy as bees / Been they, us sely men for to deceyve.' (*MerT* 2421-23) In order to establish further this connection he continues his tirade with a near repeat of the Merchant's above sentiments at the tale's commencement: 'I have a wyf, though that she povre be, / But of hir tonge, a labbyng shrewe is she, / And yet she hath an heep of vices mo; / Therof no fors! Lat alle swiche thynges go. / But wyte ye what? In conseil be it seyd, / Me reweth soore I am unto hire teyd.' (*Epi MerT* 2427-2432)

The Wife of Bath's Prologue

In this prologue Chaucer appears to be recalling the historical similarity that exists between the social consequences of the Spartan women condemned by Aristotle and, by implication, the similar general harm to King Richard's subjects now that Queen Isabel's possesses so great a political influence: 'As to giving licence to the women, it is hurtful to the end of government and to the prosperity of the State. And the first mythologists seem not without good reason to have joined Mars and Venus together; for all nations of this character appear to be greatly addicted either to the love of women or boys; for which reason it was thus at Lacedaemon; and many things in their State were done by the authority of the women. For what is the difference, if the power is in their hands,

187

whether the women rule, or whether the rulers themselves are influenced by their women? The same is the result in either case.'[98] Significantly, when the Wife informs us how she gained her mastery over the various 'five husbands' / five dispositions of King Richard, that she had achieved this through an identical combination of a Venus inspired sensuality and the ferociousness of her Mars aspect: 'Venus me yaf my lust, my likerousnesse, / And Mars yaf me my sturdy hardynesse.' (*ProWBT* 611-612)

The medieval tradition considered the male figure to be representative of the rule of reason; women signified a contradictory rule of passion. This distinction is upheld by the Parson in his summary of the *Canterbury Tales*: 'There may ye seen that deedly synne hath, first, suggestion of the feend, as sheweth hereby the naddre; and afterward, the delit of the flessh, as sheweth heere by Eve; and after that, the consentynge of resoun, as sheweth here by Adam. For trust wel, though so were that the feend tempted Eve - that is to seyn, the flessh - and the flessh hadde delit in the beautee of the fruyt defended, yet certes, til that resoun - that is to seyn, Adam - consented to the etynge of the fruyt, yet stood he in th'estaat of innocence.' (*ParsT* 331-32)

---

[98] The Politics and Economics of Aristotle, (1885), London, pp. 64-65.

The traditionally accepted scale of social degrees within God's perfectly created world would certainly have regarded female supremacy to be a corruption of the divinely ordained hierarchy: 'Thanne may men by this ordre wel discerne / That thilke Moevere stable is and eterne. / Wel may men knowe, but it be a fool, / That every part dirryveth from his hool, / For nature hath nat taken his bigynnyng / Of no partie or cantel of a thyng, / But of a thyng that parfit is and stable, / Descendynge so til it be corrumpable.' / And therefore, of his wise purveiaunce, / He hath so wel biset his ordinaunce / That speces of thynges and progressiouns / Shullen enduren by successiouns, / And nat eterne, withouten any lye.' (*KnT* 3003-15)

When the Wife of Bath rejects the biblical instruction quoted to her by one of her old husbands: 'In like manner also, that woman adorn themselves in modest apparel, with shamefacedness and sobriety; not with broided hair, or gold, or pearls, or costly array;'(*Timothy 1*, Chapter 2, verse 9) she displays the opposite conduct to that of Dorigen in the *Franklin's Tale*: 'Pryvely she fil of his accord / To take hym for hir housbonde and hir lord, / Of swich lordshipe as men han over hir wyves.' (*FranT* 741-43)

Alison of Bath's recalling of how she has mastered her three 'old' husbands displays Chaucer's humour at its very best: 'Thanne wolde I seye, Goode-lief, taak keep / How mekely looketh Wilkyn, oure sheep! / Com neer, my spouse, lat me ba thy cheke!' (*ProWBT* 431-33) My allegorical reading of this passage considers that she is here drawing an insulting comparison between King Richard's 'sheepish' disposition and the sterner authority that would have belonged to his illustrious forefather, William the Conqueror. Although 'Wilkyn' is often taken to be a diminutive of William; it's also possibly that 'kin-of-Wil' could here be the intended connection. Having addressed herself as 'Goode-lief,' the same name as is given by Harry Bailly's to his dominant wife, she recalls how these three dispositions of 'old' husbands were easily overcome with a kiss (ba) on the cheek.

The Wife's fourth husband had been of a reveller disposition, and he was therefore mastered by making 'hym of the same wode a croce.' (*ProWBT* 484) This being a time when 'I was yong and ful of ragerye, / Stibourn and strong, and joly as a pye, / How koude I daunce to an harpe smale, / And synge.'(*ProWBT* 455-58) Probably the young Alison of the *Miller's Tale* had also danced and sang to the 'sautrie' / small harp that was owned by 'hende Nicholas.' The Wife's fifth husband had been mastered by means of his having committed a grivious sin against her immature body: 'I bar hym on honde he hadde enchanted me - / My dame taughte me that soutiltee - / And eek I seyde I mette

190

of hym al nyght, / He wolde han slayn me as I lay upright, / And al my bed was ful of verray blood; / But yet I hope that ye shal do me good, / For blood bitokeneth gold, as me was taught. / And al was fals; I dremed of it right naught, / But as I followed ay my dames loore.' (*ProWBT* 575-83)

This Alison figure is intended to presents us with yet another pointer to the work's multiple connections. As in the instance when she remarks that the fifth husband had boarded with her gossip, also named Alison: 'He som tyme was a clerk of Oxenford, / And hadde left scole, and wente at hom to bord / With my gossib, dwyellynge in oure toun; / God have hir soule! Hir name was Alisoun.' (Pro*WBT* 527-30).

The Wife of Bath's Tale

The reality behind this Alison of Bath will not allow the one she claims to have been her sexual abuser to go unanswered. Because of this the Merchant's description of May as being Damyan's willing sexual partner will be countered by her own tale of a rape: 'And so bifel that this kyng Arthour / Hadde in his hous a lusty bachelor, / That on a day cam ridynge fro ryver, / And happed that, alone as he was born, / He saugh a mayde walkynge hym biforn, / Of which mayde anon, maugree hir heed, / By verray force, he rafte hire maydenhed.' (*WBT*

883-888) The Wife's subtle threat to disclose what she is implying here and elsewhere to have been her 'rape,' also appears to be hinted in her tale's King Midas anecdote concerning the difficulty wives have in keeping secret that which would bestow on 'hir housbonde so foul a name.' (*WBT* 963)

Chaucer would not have intended his readers to share the tale's knight's guilty acceptance of the Wife's conditions for their future wedded bliss: 'My lady and my love, and wyf so deere, / I put me in youre wise governance; / Cheseth yourself which may be moost pleasance / And moost honour to yow and me also.' (*WBT* 1230-33) Following from this complete submission to her implied threat, the future state of of their marriage is thus seen to have degenerated into sexual bribery: 'And thus they lyve unto hir lyves ende / In parfit joye; and Jhesu Crist us sende / Housbondes meeke, yonge, and fresh a bedde, / And grace t'overbyde hem that we wedde; / And eek I praye Jhesu shorte hir lyves / That noght wol be governed by hir wyves; / And olde and angry nygardes of dispence, / God sende hem soone verray pestilence!' (*WBT* 1257-1264)

January's refusal to consider caution in marrying without good counsel; and, following from this his subsequent failure to heed the warning of his need to thereafter control his lusts, has resulted in the creation of this formidable figure of his correction. The earlier warning given to him by

Justinus: 'Paraunter she may be youre purgatorie! / She may be Goddes meene and Goddes whippe; / Thanne shal youre soule up to hevene skippe / Swifter than dooth an arwe out of a bowe;'(*MerT* 1670-73) is seen as having been prophetic. That is the previous tale's cautioning of January: 'That ye use, as skile is and reson, / The lustes of youre wyf attemprely, / And that ye plese hire nat to amorously. / And that ye kepe yow eek from oother synne,' (*MerT* 1678-81) has become highly significant. The Wife of Bath is well aware: 'of tribulacion in mariage, / Of which I am expert in al myn age – / This is to seyn, myself have been the whippe,' (*WBT* 169-81) and her tale is clearly intended to be taken as the above described matter of 'Goddes meene and Goddes whipppe.'

The Friar's Prologue

The Friar now turns to the Wife of Bath with another hint of the name Goode-life that's given to Harry Bailly's wife and by the Wife of Bath to herself: '"Dame," quod he, "God yeve yow right good lyf! / Ye han heer touched also moot I thee, / In scole-matere greet difficultee. / Ye han seyd muche thyng right wel, I seye."' (*ProFriT* 1269-73) His further comments that such matters are however best left to authorities other than the Wife's own limited experience, and his call for frivolity rather than seriousness, suggest that this guilty disposition of King Richard feels that he needs to pass as quickly as he can from any further hints regarding the previous tale of a sexual rape: 'But, dame, heere as we ryde by the weye, / Us nedeth nat to speken but of game, / And lete auctoritees, on Goddes name, / To prechyng and to scoles of clergye.' (*FrPro* 1274-77)

The desired change of theme being immediately evidenced in his attack on the Summoner disposition: 'I wol yow of a somonour telle a game. / Pardee, ye may wel knowe by the name / That of a somonour may no good be sayd; / I praye that noon of you be yvele apayd. / A somonour is a rennere up and doun / With mandementz for fornicacioun, / And is ybet at every townes ende.' (*FrPro* 1279-1285)

The Friar's Tale

This tale's quickly moves us away from sexual matters, here the Friar describes a different form of rape: the rapacious nature of King Richard's taxation that 'made the peple pitously to synge.' (*FrT* 1316) That he has become a satanic force within his kingdom is emphatically conveyed in the frequency of those linkages that bind 'Harry Bailly' with this tale's summoner and with the devil. Nineteen times in all the word 'brother' is used to connect these last two, and the Host's surname is also oft-repeated: 'Artow thanne a bailly? ... thou art a bailly, and I am another ... syn that ye been a baillif as am I.' (*FrT* 1392-1419)

This tale's allegorical matter should present us with no difficulty. Having driven the royal treasury into the mire of insolvency, the tale's carter representative of King Richard responds by striking out at his horses: 'The cartere smoot and cryde as he were wood, / "Hayt, Brok! Hayt, Scot! / What spare ye for the stones? / The feend," quod he, "yow fecche, body and bones, / As foerforthly as evere were ye foled, / So muche wo as I have with you tholded! / The devel have al, bothe hors and cart and hey!"' (*FrT* 1542-47) Further evidence of how far-reaching in detail these allegories are is found in the names chosen for these horses: both 'Broc' and 'Scot' convey significant figurative pointers. 'Broc' implies 'menace;' and 'scot'was a tax that paid for the services of a bailiff; here, these terms present us with dominant pointers to the figure of Harry Bailly. Within the tale's ongoing allegorical framework they imply that this carter's financial difficulties will be overcome by means of King Richard threatening his subjects with an increased level of taxation.

Although at that time not sincerely intended: 'The carl spak oon thing, but he thoghte another;' (*FrT* 1568) the carter's threat to be free of his

195

responsibilities: 'The devel have al, bothe hors and cart and hey!' (*FrT* 1547) may be grounded on an earlier historical episode in which King Richard had threatened his lords with the threat of his abdication. Certainly, on becoming Henry of Lancaster's prisoner in 1399, he expressed a wish to renounce his royal responsibilities. However, at that later period the political circumstances were very different; then possessing powerful supporters and fearing later reprisals if the revengeful Richard was allowed to regain his kingly power, Henry took full advantage of his words and out of necessity had himself crowned King Henry IV of England. Not surprisingly in this tale's hint of an earlier episode of threatened abdication we find that when the cart is eventually brought out of the mire, the Devil's confident prediction that the carter is not serious in this threatening is immediately confirmed.

It is important here to understand that the congratulations issued by the carter are to be read as self-praises. They are not as is now believed to be directed towards the horses: 'That was wel twight, myn owene lyard boy. / I pray God save thee, and Seinte Loy! / Now is my cart out of the slow, pardee!' (*FrT* 1562-64) 'Twight' / to disparage, as in 'And evermore he did him sharpely twight.'[99] 'Lyard' is probably another of Chaucer's compound

---

[99] Spenser, Poetical Works, Eds. J. C. Smith and E. de Selincourt, Oxford University Press, (1970), p. 302.

words: 'ly' being a derivitive of the Latin word *laicus* / pertaining to the people, and the termination 'ard' comes into the English language from the German word *hart* / hard. In the majority of its usages this suffix is applied in the negative sense: dull<u>ard</u>, cow<u>ard</u>, lagg<u>ard</u>. Celebrated as a competent master of the French royal treasury, the insertion of Saint Eloy's name into the above passage indicates King Richard's contentment over his own 'Eloy-like' replenishing of his royal treasury.

The 'twelf pens' that the tale's summoner demands from the tale's poor widow; a sum mentioned five times, appears to represent King Richard's insistence on the collection of his infamous poll-tax. This was a tax that by the winter of 1380-81 put on each village an average sum of one shilling a head: one shilling equalled twelve pence. "'Twelf pens!" quod she, "Now, lady Seinte Marie / So wisly help me out of care and synne, / This wyde world thogh that I sholde wynne, / Ne have I nat twelf pens withinne myn hoold.'" (*FrT* 1604-07) When this 'widow' figure fails to pay him the required taxation the summoner's insists on other forms of compensation: 'Pay me, quod he, or by the sweete Seinte Anne, / As I wol bere awey thy newe panne / For dette which thou owest me of old.' (*FrT* 1613-15) The historical reality here being that King Richard had ousted the local collectors, and when the poorest of his subjects could not afford the sums he demanded from them, he presented his sergeants-at-arms with the power to commence a house-to-house survey.

The danger that such a royal tyranny posed to the reign's security is evidenced in the widow's expression of anger on being robbed of her frying pan and of those other essentials she required to keep herself alive: "'Unto the devel blak and rough of hewe / Yeve I thy body and my panne also!" / And whan the devel herde hire cursen so / Upon hir knees, he seyde in this manere, / "Now, Mabely, myn owene mooder deere, / Is this youre wyl in ernest that ye seye?" / "The devel," quod she, "so fecche hym er he deye, / And panne and al, but he wol hym repente!"' (*FrT* 1622-29). King Richard failed to repent such forms of tyranny towards his subjects, and later in the reign he was deservedly dethroned.

This tale of implied royal avarice closes on the hope of the summoner's correction; and with this consideration the Friar issues a plea: 'And God, that maked after his ymage / Mankynde, save and gyde us, alle and some, / And leve thise somonours goode men bicome!' (*FrT* 1642-44) It's suggested that Christ, in his role of defender of the downtrodden, will eventually intervene on behalf of Richard's subjects: 'The leoun sit in his awayt always / To sle the innocent, if that he may, / Disposeth ay youre hertes to withstonde / The feend, that you wolde make thrall and bonde. / He may nat tempte yow over youre might, / For Crist wol be youre champion and knight.' (*FrT* 1659-62) By means of Henry of Lancaster's intervention in 1399, such as this tale's description of the rapacious cruelty of King Richard II's rule was eventually brought to its conclusion.

The Summoner's Tale

In this next tale we find that King Richard's personality has been divided between the prudent Thomas and the spendthrift Friar John dispositions. The unknown saint of this tale named by the friar: 'And by that lord that clepid is Seint Yve,' (*SumT* 1943) suggests a punning on the word 'give.' 'Yve' is an oft-repeated word within the tale: 'Yif us a busshel whete, malt, or reye, / A Goddes kechyl, or a trype of chese, / Or elles what yow lyst, we may nat cheese; / A Goddes halfpeny, or a masse peny, / Or yif us of youre brawn, if ye have eny.' (*SumT* 1746-53) This same word is repeated later and stressed by being placed at the line headings: 'Thomas, that jape nys nat worth a myte. / Youre maladye is for we han to lyte. / A, yif that covent half a quarter otes! / A, yif that covent foure and twenty grotes! / A, yif that frère a peny, and lat hym go!' (*SumT* 1961-1965)

The tale's opposites of the friar and daun John are indicated in the wife's remark to the friar that her 'child' had died 'withinne thise wykes two, / Soone after that ye wente out of this toun.' (*SumT* 1852-53) I take this mention of 'child' to figure the biblical meaning of one who exhibits the unthinking characteristics of a young person. In Saint John's Gospel the Christian brotherhood is twice addressed as 'little children;' this being a description that alludes to the less perceptive members of the community; 'Fathers' signified the more enlightened. From such as these opposites the tale's theme becomes obvious. Immediately following the friar's arrival the wife complains to him of her husband's mood of seriousness, and couples this with his lack of sexual interest: "'Now, by youre leve, o deere sire,' quod she, / Chideth him weel, for seinte Trinitee! / He is as angry as a pissemyre, / Though that he have al that he kan desire, / Though I hym wrye a-nyght and make hym warm, / And over hym leye my leg outher myn arm, / He groneth lyk oure boor, lith in oure sty. / Oother desport right noon of hym have I; / I may nat plese hym in no maner cas.'" (*SumT* 1823-1831)

Here the tale's wife is obviously referring to that time when sexual bribery cannot entice her husband away from concern over the consequences of the previous 'child-like' neglect of his financial affairs. That time when the sexually exhausted daun

Thomas aspect has gained ascendancy within the king's personality; then, neither the wife's complaining or the grasping daun John disposition are able to separate him from his need to be careful over his expenditure: 'And whan this sike man felte this frère / Aboute his tuwel gope there and heere, / Amydde his hand he leet the frère a fart; / Ther nys no capul, drawynge in a cart, / That myghte have lete a fart of swich a soun.'(*SumT* 2147-2151)

The Shipman's Tale

This is another tale that responds to the theme of the previous: 'A marchant whilom dwelled at Seint-Denys, / That riche was, for which men helde hym wys. / A wyf he hadde of excellent beautee; / And compaignable and revelous was she, / Which is a thyng that causeth more dispence / Than worth is al the chiere and reverence / That men hem doon at festes and at daunces. / Swiche salutaciouns and contenaunces / Passen as dooth a shadwe upon the wal; / But wo is hym that payen moot for al! / The sely housbonde, algate he moot paye, / He moot us clothe, and he moot us arraye, / Al for his owene worshipe richely, / In which array we daunce jolily.' (*ShipT* 1- 14)

Previous readers often misconstrue these opening lines: 'The tale may originally have been intended for another narrator ... the pronouns 'we' and 'us' suggest a married female speaker ... the shipman may be mimicking a female speaker.' (*Riverside*, p. 910) Such mistaken interpretations are bound to appear when King Richard is not recognised as being the hidden reality behind the Shipman; that is, the above 'we' and 'us' are then seen to be forms of address that has for a long time been held to be of traditional usage by kings and other potentates. As early as 1204-15 we find evidence of King John resorting to the royal 'we' in his official documents.

Following our awareness of the speaker's royal presence the above is readily understood to imply those extravagant feasts and dances held at the royal court: 'The sely housbonde' (peasanty) is expected to endure 'swich dispence;' but if they cannot then the more powerful lords of the realm / (another) must 'payen for oure cost, / Or lene us gold ... and that is perilous.' (*ShipT* 18-19) We should not too readily be thrown off course by the above word 'housbonde;' not only did it signify a man joined to a woman in marriage, it also referred to the peasant tiller of the soil. Husband–land being an old term for a division of land containing twenty-six acres, an area that could be tilled with one plough or mowed with the husbandman's scythe.

The prudent 'goode man' Thomas disposition of the *Summoner's Tale* has here been replaced in this tale by the 'goode man' chapman, another representative of King Richard that carefully calculates his money and warns his wife of the need to keep 'a thrifty houshold.' (*ShipT* 246) The Friar John role of the preceding tale is taken up by this tale's Daun John the monk; this being another religious figure named 'John,' and he will repay the prudent Thomas disposition of the previous tale for his insult. This 'noble' monk: 'I trowe a thritty wynter he was oold,' (*ShipT* 26) approximates King Richard's age around the time shortly following his second marriage; Queen Isabel's childhood also appears to be hinted in the tale's 'mayde child ... yet under the yerde' (*ShipT* 95-96) that accompanies the chapman's wife in her 'privas' / private walk through the garden.

The chapman's wife is connected to the Wife of Bath through such links as Alison of Bath's angry: 'Peter! I shrew yow;' (*WBT* 446) having being given a near repeat in this tale's: 'Peter! it am I.' (*ShipT* 214) The more obvious tie-in between these two being their descriptions of what constitutes an ideal husband: 'Jhesu Crist us sende / Housbondes meeke, yonge, and fressh abedde, / And grace t'overbyde hem that we wedde; / And eek I pray Jhesu shorte hir lyves / That wol nat be governed by hir wyves; / And olde and angry nygardes of dispence, / God sende hem soone verray pestilence!' (*WBT* 1258-64) The chapman's wife holds the same opinion: 'But yet me greveth moost his nygardye. / And wel ye woot that wommen naturally / Desiren thynges sixe as wel as I: / They wolde that hir housbondes sholde be / Hardy and wise, and riche, and therto free, / And buxom unto his wyf and fressh abedde.' (*ShipT* 172-77).

Another clue of the tale's hidden royalty, one which often misdirects previous critics, comes in the chapman's mentioned need to occasionally 'pleye / a pilgrimage.' (*ShipT* 233-34) This comment being a rather obvious hint of Richard's frequent need to emphasize his semi-divine position as God's earthly representative. This king would not have been the first or the last monarch that resorted to the propaganda of a devotional pilgrimage as a means of negating the rebellious instincts of his impoverished subjects. Inevitably, those who insist on providing a literal reading of this text will find the above 'pleye a pilgrimage' troublesome: 'A difficult passage. For different interpretations, see Baugh and Copland: pleye / A pilgrimage may mean either that merchants seek relaxation on pilgrimages ... or to go away on pilgrimages in order to escape creditors.'(*Riverside* p. 912).

Within this tale the re-emergence of sexual desire within King Richard's psyche is conveyed in the chapman's requests that daun John 'com to Seinte Denys to pleye / With him and his wyf a day or tweye.' (*ShipT* 59-60) Such a request presents an identical allegorical purpose to that I have already given in my reading of the earlier corrupting Perotheus influence: 'A worthy duc that highte Perotheus, / That felawe was unto duc Theseus / Syn thilke day that they were children lite, / Was come to Atthenes his felawe to visite, / And for to pleye as he was wont to do.' (*KnT* 1191-95)

The following lines imply a dire warning to the tale's chapman of the health perils that are to be associated with generating sexual heat on a full stomach of rich food and alcohol: 'Who was so welcome as my lord daun John / Oure deere cosyn, ful of curteisye? / With hym broghte he a jubbe of malvesye, / And eek another ful of fyn vernage, / And volatyl, as ay was his usage. / And thus I lete hem ete and drynke and pleye, / This marchant and this monk, a day or tweye.' (*ShipT* 68-74) After the rich food and wine it's probably the chapman's penis that is being described to be standing so: 'And after-dyner daun John sobrely / This chapman took apart, and prively / He seyde hm thus: "Cosyn, it standeth so, / That wel I se to Brugges wol ye go. / God and Seint Austyn spede yow and gyde!"' (*ShipT* 255-259) That is, the impending act of sexual intercourse has the monk warning the chapman to consider the combined dangers of gluttony and drinking as he 'rides' towards Bruges: 'I prey yow, cosyn, wisely that ye ryde. / Governeth yow also of youre diete / Attemprely, and namely in this hete.' (*ShipT* 255-62)

The word 'chaffare' held the dual meaning of 'merchandise' and 'chafe' / warmth; here it probably implies such heat as that generated through the friction of sexual intercourse. His having received 'an hundred frankes' from the merchant disposition, a sum that's used in order to ensure that he is favoured with sexual intercourse with the wife: 'He sholde al nyght / Have hire in his armes bolt upright;' (*ShipT* 315-16) it's not surprising that we find the monk's departure from the tale is immediately followed by the chapman's return with a complaint to the wife that 'chaffare is so deere.' (*ShipT* 328)

Chaucer's disgust at his king's beast-like sexual behaviour with the child queen is surely implied in this tale's oft-repeated use of animal imagery. The chapman lives 'at Seint-Denys:' (*ShipT* 1) a 'den' is the lair of animals, as in 'She dorste wilde beestes dennes seke.' (*MkT* 2263) Daun John the monk swears by 'Seint Martyn;' (*ShipT* 148) mart / market place, a word drawn from Martinmas, that time when whatever animal was due to be slaughtered for winter provision could be bought. Being mentioned four times in the tale the word 'bruges' suggests a compound of *bru* / brute and the French *ges*, as in *gesir* / lying down; that is, the 'brutish' monk disposition and the wife lay themselves down to copulate 'al nyght' while the chapman disposition is said to be at 'Bruges.' The money Daun John the monk requests from the chapman, the amount which he pays the chapman's wife for the sexual favour he receives, is required in order to purchase 'certein beestes.' (*ShipT* 272) A purchase that's to be conducted that night: 'For yet to-nyght thise beestes moot I bye.' (*ShipT* 278)

In this tale the Shipman present us with an allegorical description of how the hidden reality behind the wife has succeeded in encouraging her husband's Daun John / monkish disposition, and how that sexual act enables her to receive the 'hundred frankes' (*ShipT* 181) required to pay for the clothes she claims to have been bought for the chapman's 'honour, myself for to arraye.' (*ShipT* 179) Not surprisingly the tale's animal imagery is also found to have been convincingly underlined at this tale's ending. If the following does not convey such an allegorical significance as I maintain, it seems somewhat unusual that Chaucer has the following from the Host at its close: 'The monk putte in the mannes hood an ape, / And in his wyves eek, by Seint Austyn! / Draweth no monkes moore unto youre in.' (*ShipT* 440-42)

Prologue of the Prioress's Tale

The real-life identities behind these various pilgrims often argue over the responsibility for the immoral act that resulted in the child Queen Isabel's loss of her virginity. That is we are presented with hints of personal innocence being claimed by hidden representatives of either King Richard or Queen Isabel. I believe that this prologue and tale conveys Queen Isabel's powerful response to the Shipman's implied descriptions that it was she, figured as being the chapman's wife, who had prostituted herself for monetary gain. The Prioress will now counter this assertion with the telling of King Richard's monkish disposition having been guilty of betraying her childhood innocence.

The Prioress's Tale

As when the age of Virginia of the *Physician's Tale* is changed from that found in the source to 'twelve yeer was and tweye' in order that complement Queen Anne's age on her arrival in England; here, we find that Chaucer has changed this tale's child age from that found in the originals to Queen Isabel's seven years on her marriage to King Richard: 'The child is ordinarily ten in the analogues.' (*Riverside*, p. 915) A pointer to Queen Isabel's claimed English nickname of 'Little

Queen' also appears to be implied in the tale's constant repetition of the word 'little:' this 'litel body' is a 'litel child,' a 'litel clergeon' that learns hymns from a 'litel book' in 'a litel scole.'

The grain taken from the child's tongue by the monk: 'That was an hooly man, / As monkes been or elles oght be,' (*PrT* 642-43) has been given a variety of interpretations. In this response to the *Shipman's Tale* 'the Prioress is implying that the sexual act described in the previous tales was not one of consent but rather the forced removal of the 'grain of her virginity' from her innocent self: 'This hooly monk ... took awey the greyn.'(PrT 670-71) Although her tale retains the Christian promise of redemption: 'My litel child, now wol I fecche thee, / Whan that the greyn is fro thy tonge ytake. / Be nat agast; I wol thee nat forsake;' (*PrT* 667-69) following the loss of her virginial purity the one who had earlier in her tale sung '*O Alma* loude and cleere,' (*PrT* 655) informs us that she has now become one of life's 'synful folk unstable.' (*PrT* 687).

Sir Thopas

In this tale Chaucer retaliates against the Host insulting comment of his elfish appearance: 'This were a popet in an arm t'enbrace / For any womman, smal and fair of face. / He semeth elvyssh

209

by his contenaunce.' (Pro*Thop* 694-96) Let us assume here that the six-footer tall figure of the Host has just finished listening to the *Prioress's Tale*; glancing around the pilgrims he notices the small in stature figure of Chaucer and immediately follows this with the jest that he would be an ideal person for the Prioress to embrace: that he is also small, like a child or a doll; the French word being *poupette*, Latin *pupa*, a child or a doll.

Probably this is why in this tale we have here another example of Chaucer humourously responding to such an insult from a representative figure of King Richard. That is he now counters with a mocking hint that implies how the reality behind the Host has himself married such a small and therefore 'elf-like' bride: 'An elf-queene wol I love, ywis, / For in this world no woman is / Worthy to be my make / In towne; / Alle othere wommen I forsake, / And to an elf-queene I me take / By dale and eek by downe!' (*Thop* 790-796) Not only this, it may also be adding the following slight of Richard occasionally possessing a painted Thopas-like appearance: 'Sire Thopas wax a doghty swayn; / Whit was his face as payndemayn, / His lippes rede as rose' (*Thop* 724-26) Not surprisingly such derision over King Richard's Thopas-like looks, and his choice of an 'elvyssh' wife, induces the following angry interruption from the Host:

'Thy drasty rymyng is nat worth a toord!' (*Thop* 948)

Because of this Chaucer will attempt to ensure that he be allowed to complete his next tale without any disruption. That is his telling of the direct and important political counselling found in his tale of Melibee: 'I wol yow telle a litel thyng in prose / That oghte liken yow, as I suppose, / Or elles, certes, ye been to daungerous. / It is a moral tale virtuous / Al be it told somtyme in sondry wyse / Of sondry folk, as I shal yow devyse.' (*Thop* 937-942) Before commencing with this second attempt of a tale Chaucer requests that he be allowed this time to complete its important sentence: 'And therefore herkneth what that I shal seye, / And lat me tellen al my tale, I preye.' (*Thop* 965-66)

The Tale of Melibee

I read this tale's allegory to be a portrayal of King Richard's furious reaction on finding his belief in the absolute power possessed by the royal prerogative having been opposed by the intervention of the Appellant Council in their 1388 removal and execution of those amongst his courtiers they considered to be a dangerous influence regarding the safety of his rule. This tale not only describes the king's anger over the intervention, it also expresses his initial intention of gaining a military revenge against the three leading Appellants: Gloucester, Arundel and Warwick; those that had for a short time curtailed his extravagances and his listening to the advice of the flatterers at his court.

Probably the inability of previous readers to understand this rather obvious interpretation has resulted from their critical failure to differentiate between the tale's mention of the 'three enemys of mankynde;' that is 'the flesh, the world, and the devil,' and King Richard / Melibee's three leading figures of opposition mentioned above. That these represent two different groups of 'three' is made abundantly clear at the tale's close when, having been so advised by Melibee's wife, his three adversaries arrive at his court and 'the wiseste of hem thre,' (*Mel* 1816) submits himself and his two companions to receive the forgiving oaths of their lord. The notion that such a wise counsellor as Prudence would create a peace treaty between her husband and 'the three enemys of mankynde' is not a sensible reading of the tale.

From the historical standpoint this is probably the most detailed tale of the *Canterbury* series. The figure of Melibee, 'myghty and riche,' immediately suggests King Richard; and the tale Prudence implies Queen Anne. The refusal of the appellants to heed the pleadings of Queen Anne, that they spare the lives of Richard's friends, results in the figurative description of Prudence having been 'betten' by Melibee's 'olde foes.' This having in turn resulted in Melibee's 'doghter which that called was Sophie' (wisdom) having suffered 'fyve mortal woundes in fyve sondry places – this is to seyn, in hir feet, in hire handes, in hir erys, in hir nose, and in hire mouth ... Whan Melibeus returned was into his hous, and saugh al this meschief, he, lyk a mad man rentynge his clothes, gan to wepe and crie.' (*Mel* 967-973) Queen Anne is reported to have been on her knees pleading before the appellants that they spare the life of Simon de Burley, the former childhood tutor and close friend of King Richard's minority.

From here onwards in the tale, in her role as a wise and prudent confidant of her husband, Queen Anne seeks to lessen her husband's anger: 'Prudence, his wyf, as ferforth as she dorste, bisoght hym of his wepyng for to stynte, / but nat forthy he gan to crie and wepen evere lenger the moore.' (*Mel* 974-975) Rather than his foolish choice of plunging the country into civil war, she counsels him to assess his own faults at that earlier time, and from his consideration of these to make his peace with God and with the appellants. The difference between Melibee's foolish ranting and the wise counselling he receives from Prudence suggests that from here onwards her words to the 'mad man rentynge his clothes' are the sentiments expressed by such a person as the country's most successful peacemaker: 'This noble wyf Prudence remembered hire upon the sentence of Ovide, in his book that cleped is the *Remedie of Love*, where as he seith, / "He is a fool that destourbeth the mooder to wepen in the deeth of hire child til she have wept hir fille as for a certein tyme, / And thanne shal man doon his diligence with amyable wordes hire to reconforte, and preyen hire of hir wepyng for to stynte."' (*Mel* 976- 978)

The *Melibee* appears to present us with an approximate account of a real debate that could have taken place between King Richard and Queen Anne. We find that Melibee: 'So greet a lord ... youre heigh lordshipe ... your gracious lordshipe;' the one who initially favoured retaliation through war instead of an attempted lawful correction of this political opposition, is eventually persuaded by his wife to overcome the dark mood of anger he feels towards those he believed to be his mortal enemies: "I conseille yow," quod she, "above alle thynges, that ye make pees bitwene God and yow, / and beth reconsiled unto hym and to his grace. / For, as I have seyd yow heer biforn, God hath suffred yow to have this tribulacioun and disese for youre synnes. / And if ye do as I sey yow, God wol sende youre adversaries unto yow / and maken hem fallen at youre feet, redy to do youre wyl and youre

214

comandementz. / For Salomon seith, Whan the condicioun of man is plesaunt and likynge to God, / he chaungeth the hertes of the mannes adversaries and constreyneth hem to biseken hym of pees and of grace. / And I prey yow lat me speke with youre adversaries in privee place, / for they shul nat knowe that it be of youre wyl or of youre assent. / And thanne, whan I knowe hir wil and hire entente, I may conseille yow the moore seurely" ... "Dame", quod Melibee, "dooth youre wil and youre likynge; / for I putte me hoolly in youre disposicoun and ordinaunce.'" (*Mel* 1714-1725).

Prudence reminds her husband that he has previously been possessed by an excessive love of sensuality, and with this in the forefront of her counselling she attempts to point out and thereby correct his previous behaviour: 'Thy name is Melibee; this is to seyn, a man that drynketh hony. / Thou hast ydronke so muchel hony of sweete temporeel richesses, and delices and honours of this world / that thou art dronken and hast forgeten Jhesu Crist thy creatour. / Thou ne hast nat doon to hym swich honour and reverence as thee oughte, / ne hast nat wel ytaken kep to the wordes of Ovide, that seith. / "Under the hony of the goodes of the body is hyd the venym that sleeth the soule." And Salomon seith, "If thou hast founden hony, ete of it that suffiseth, / for it thou ete of it out of mesure, thou shalt spewe and be nedy and povre." / And

215

peraventure Crist hath thee in despit, and hath turned awey fro thee his face and his eeris of misericorde, / and hath suffred that thou hast been punysshed in the manere that thow hast ytrespassed.' (*Mel* 1410-19)

She informs him further that the intervention of those he now believes to be his adversaries could be Christ's way of correcting him for permitting wordly pride to enter his soul and influence him into the ways of evil: 'Thou hast doon synne agayn oure Lord Crist, / For certes, the three enemys of mankynde - that is to seyn, the flessh, the feend, and the world - / thou hast suffred hem entre in to thyn herte wilfully by the wyndowes of thy body, / and hast nat defended thyself suffisantly agayns hire assautes and hire temptaciouns so that they han wounded thy soule in fyve places; / this is to seyn, the deedly synnes that been entred into thyn herte by thy fyve wittes. / And in this same manere oure Lord Crist hath woold and suffred that thy three enemys been entred into thyn house by the wyndowes / and han ywounded thy doghter in the forseyde manere.' (*Mel* 120-26) Notice it is 'thy' daughter, not 'our' daughter that she mentions here: it's King Richard's wisdom that's being referred to as Sophie his daughter.

How closely Chaucer may have followed real events in this narrative of Prudence's counselling cannot be determined from this brief outline of what

216

I consider to be the tale's allegorical format. Being of a revengeful nature, and undoubtedly furious over what he took to have been their treasonable actions against his royal prerogative, it seems that King Richard may well have favoured a reckless and bloody retaliation against these same lords in 1389. Undoubtedly, the greatest difficulty in resolving this matter peacefully was the appellant awareness of Richard's untrustworthiness. Could they rely on the royal assurances being granted to them by the revengeful King Richard?

Such an allegorical reading of the tale as I have proposed above may well indicate how it was that eventually King Richard's thoughts of retribution against the appellants was to be peacefully settled: 'Thanne dame Prudence, whan she saugh the goode wyl of hir housbonde, delibered and took avys in hirself, / thinkinge how she myghte brynge this need unto a good conclusioun and to a good ende. / And whan she saugh hir tyme, she sente for thise adversaries to come unto hire into a pryvee place / and shewed wisely unto hem the grete goodes that comen of pees / and the grete harmes and perils that been in werre, / and seyde to hem in a goodly manere how that hem oghten have greet repentaunce / of the injurie and wrong that they hadden doon to Melibee hir lord.' (*Mel* 1724-32)

This tale's description of Queen Anne's wise and persuasive counselling of both sides in the confrontation was probably such that eventually ensured the matter of their essential trust in Richard's forgiveness being acceptable: 'And nathelees I conseille yow that ye mystruste nat my lord, / for I woot wel and knowe verraily that he is debonaire and meeke, large, curteys, / and nothyng desirous ne coveitous of good ne richesse. / For ther nys nothyng in this world that he desireth, save oonly worshipe and honour. / Forthermoore I knowe wel and am right seur that he shal nothyng doon in this nede withouten my conseil, / and I shal so werken in this cause that by the grace of oure Lord God ye shul be reconciled unto us. / Thanne seyden they with o voys, "Worshipful lady, we putten us and oure goodes al fully in youre wil and disposicoun, / and be redy to comen, what day that it liketh unto youre goodnesse, / that we mowe fulfille the wille of yow and of my lord Melibee"' (*Mel* 1759-68).

In 1388-89 Queen Anne succeeded in turning her husband away from his revengeful course: 'Whanne Melibee hadde herd the grete skiles and resouns of dame Prudence, and hire wise informaciouns and techynges. / his herte gan enclyne to the wil of his wif, considerynge hir trewe entente, / and conformed hym anon and assented fully to werken after hir conseil, / and thonked God,

218

of whom precedeth al vertu and alle goodnesse, that hym sente a wyf of so greet discrecioun.' (*Mel.* 1870-73) She had also provided the three leading appellants with such confidence as enabled them to accept that under her guidance he could be trusted to honour his promises of forgiveness and reconcilliation: 'Wherfore I receive yow to my grace / and foryeve yow outrely alle the offenses, injuries, and wronges that ye have doon again me and myne, / to this effect and to this ende, that God of his endeless mercy / wole at the tyme of oure diynge foryeven us oure giltes that we han trespassed to hym in this wrecched world. / For douteless, if we be sory and repentant of the synnes and giltes which we han trespassed in the sight of oure Lord God, / he is so free and so merciable, / that he wole foryeven us oure giltes / and bryngen us to the blisse that nevere hath ende." Amen.' (*Mel.* 1881-88)

Disastrously for the former appellants, and eventually for the king himself, following Queen Anne's early death in 1394 these same oaths of forgiveness were revoked by the reckless Richard; and from that time onwards, probably also due to his impoverished treasury, he set about the destruction of those he considered to have been his former opposition.

The Prologue to the Monk's Tale

Not surprisingly the Host aspect of King Richard follows this tale with a comparison of his present wife's foolish aggressiveness: 'Oure Hooste seyde, "As I am faithful man, / And by that precious corpus Madrian, / I hadde levere than a barel ale / That Goodelief, my wyf, hadde herd this tale! / ... I woot wel she wol do me slee som day / Som neighebor, and thane go my way; / For I am perilous with knyf in honde."' (*Pro Mkt* 1891-1919) This prologue contains Chaucer's humour at its very best. Notice the above Host reference to himself as being a 'faithful man,' and with this the mastery he declares his wife to have over his behaviour: 'Al be it that I dar nat hire withstonde, / For she is byg in armes, by my feith.' (*Pro MkT* 1920-210) The above name of 'Madrian,' the otherwise unknown saint mentioned here, I take to be a compound of the English word 'mad' and the earlier French word 'rian / queen.' When this is compared to the wise counselling of his first queen, that of his second queen is correctly described as such as is being given to him by his 'mad queen.'

The Host's attempts to discover the Monk's lineage appears to be a probing of whether the Monk is of a similar disposition to daun John in the *Shipman's Tale* or to the Thomas figure in the *Summoner's Tale*: 'Wher shal I calle yow my lord daun John, / Or daun Thomas, or elles daun Albon? / Of what hous be ye, by youre fader kyn?' (*MkT* 1929-31) He eventually closes this line of questioning on the above : 'or elles daun Albon?' / Albon from the Latin *albus* / white, this being a word that signified the white cliffs of Dover. Chaucer has the following in his short poem that's titled *Complaint to his* Purse: 'O conquerour of Brutes Albyon, / Which that by lyne and free eleccion / Been verray kyng....' (*Riverside*, p. 656)

The Monk's Tale

This tale commences with the seriousness of the Monk's theme: 'I wol biwaille in manere of tragedie / The harm of hem that stoode in heigh degree, / And fillen so that ther nas no remedie / To brynge hem out of hir adversitee. / But certain, whan that Fortune list to flee, / Ther may no man the cours of hire withholde. / Let no man truste on blynd prosperitee; / Be war by thise ensamples trewe and olde.' (*MkT* 1991-1998)

Not only does it present evidence that no position of power can be considered absolutely secure; and it also demonstrates that the prideful behaviour by those in high office can often hasten the turning of Fortune's Wheel against their rule: 'Now fil it so that Fortune liste no lenger / The hye pryde of Nero to cherice, / For though that he were strong, yet was she strenger. / She thoughte thus: "By God! I am to nyce / To sete a man that is fulfild of vice / In heigh degree, and emperour hym calle. / By God, out of his sete I wol hym trice; / Whan he leest weneth, soonest shal he falle." / The peple roos upon hym on a nyght / For his defaute.' (*Mkt* 2519-2528)

It may well be significant that this tale's lengthy description of Seneca's attempts to turn the tyrannous Nero away from such behaviour implies Chaucer's similar attempts with his king: 'In yowthe a maister hadde this emperour / To teche hym letterure and curteisye, / For of moralitee he was the flour, / As in his tyme.' (*MkT* 2495-98) That is Chaucer could well be hinting his own equally futile attempts to instruct his sovereign into a form of conduct more befitting that of a lord towards his subjects: 'This Seneca, of which that I devyse, / By cause Nero hadde of hym swich drede, / For he fro vices wolde hym ay chastise / Discreetly, as by word and nat by dede / "Sire," wolde he seyn, "an emperor moot nede / Be virtuous and hate tirannye."' (*MkT* 2503-08)

Whether it be the above mentioned Nero, or the many other such examples of the mighty that fall from power when they believe themselves most secure: such historical figures as Alexander the Great and Julius Caesar; or even the later in time examples of Peter of Cyprus in 1369; Peter of

Spain, King of Castile and Leon, (1350-69); and in May 1385 Bernabo, Viscount of Milan, that died in his prison cell, the Monk presents a long list of such examples. Finally, when he highlights the proud reign of Croesus, the last King of Lydia; (560-546 B. C.) he arrives at the most significant example for the telling of the next tale. Considering the equally prideful nature of King Richard II's reign, it's readily understandable that this tale's list of tragedies should draw to its close with the stark warning found in this final example: 'Cresus, the proude kyng; / His roial trone myghte hym nat availle. / Tragedies noon oother maner thyng / Ne kan in syngyng crie ne biwaille / But that Fortune alwey wol assaille / With unwar strook the regnes that been proude, / For whan men trusteth hire, thanne wel she faille, / And covere hire bright face with a clowde.' (*MkT* 2759-2766)

The Prologue of the Nun's Priest's Tale

This is another significant prologue, one that commences with Chaucer the Knight's solemn interruption of the Monk: "'Hoo!" quod the Knyght; "Good sire, namoore of this! / That ye han seyd is right ynough, ywis, / And muchel moore; for litel hevynesse / Is right ynough to muche folk, I gesse. / I seye for me, it is a great disese, / Whereas men han been in greet welthe and ese, / To heeren of hire sodeyn fal, allas! / And the contrarie is joye and greet solas. / As whan a man hath been in povre estaat, / And clymbeth up and wexeth fortunate, / And there abideth in prosperitee. / Swich thyng is gladsom, as it thynketh me, / And of swich thyng were goodly for to telle.'" (*Pro NPT* 2767-2779)

The Host's unease over what he has just heard, and with this his declared inability to comprehend such as the Monk's directness of presentation greatly increases the likelihood of King Richard's future fall from such power and privilege as he foolishly considers to be entirely dependent on Fortune's favour: "'Ye,'" quod oure Hooste, "by Seint Poules belle! / Ye seye right sooth; this Monk he clappeth lowde. / He spak how Fortune covered with a clowde / I not nevere what; and als of a tragedie / Right now ye herde, and pardee, no remedie / It is for to biwaille ne compleyne / That that is doon; and also it is a peyne, / As ye han seyd, to heere of hevynesse. / Sire Monk, namoore of this, so God yow blesse! / Youre tale anoyeth al this compaignye. / Swich talking is nat worth a boterflye, / For therinne is ther no desport ne game.'"(*Pro NPT* 2780-2791) We find that in the next tale the foolish Chauntecleer believes that his listening to flattery is 'worth a boterflye.'

The Nun's Priest's Tale

The allegorical interpretation I propose for this tale will in part follow the drift of such a political reading as I have mentioned that Professor Hotson proposed in his reading of this tale; but unlike his it will be consistent with the unfolding historical reality, and should therefore be the more convincing. My intention here is to demonstrate that although Professor Hotson was correct in his reading of the tale as containing an allusion to the Duke of Gloucester's murder at Calais, because he had been mistaken in his understanding of the real-life connections, his unfolding of the tale's relevant historical details are incorrect.

Keeping to what has gone before in my appraisal of the other tales, I claim Chauntecleer to be a representative of King Richard's royal presence: 'real (royal) he was,' (*NPT* 3176) 'roial, as a prince is in his halle;' (*NPT* 3184) Chauntecleer the cock is introduced to us 'sat on his perche, that was in the halle.' (*NPT* 2884) Pertelote the hen implies an obvious stand-in for Queen Isabel. As is found in allegories, the 'poor widow' represents the impoverished peasantry and the fox signifies the presence of the flatterers that attended the royal court: 'Then betidith it that, yif thou seest a wyght that be transformed into vices, thow ne mayst nat wene that he be a man ... and if he be a pryve awaytour yhid, and rejoiseth hym to ravyssche be wiles, thow schalt seyn hym lik to the fox whelpes.'[100] Within such an allegory as I propose, the widow's yard: 'A yeerd she hadde, enclosed al aboute / With stikkes, and a drye dyche without,' (*NPT* 2847-48) could imply such as Windsor Castle; a fortress with its defensive ditch and a stout palisade that followed the shape of the hill as it formed the outer defences.

The word 'widow' derives from the Latin *viduus*; fem. *vidua* / bereft. This term being a biblical symbol for the downtrodden within society: 'Woe unto you, scribes and Pharisees, hypocrites! For you devour widows' houses.' (Matt. 23: 14) This tale's 'poor widow' endures a harsh economic existence: 'This wydwe, of which I telle yow my tale, / Syn thilke day that she was last a wyf / In pacience ladde a ful symple lyf, / For litel was hir catel and hire rente.' (*NPT* 2824-27) A later sixteenth-century dramatist presents a 'widow' figure in his portrayal of the poverty-stricken:

---

[100] *Riverside*, *Boece*, Book IV, Metrum 2, ll. 101 ff.

King John:

I have worn the crown and wroght
victoriously;
And now do purpose, by practice and by
study,
To reform the laws and set men in good
order;
That true justice may be had in every border.

England (*Vidua*):

Then I trust your grace will weigh
a poor widow's cause,
Ungodly used, as ye shall know in short
clause.[101]

Also being personified as a widow in another
play of this later period, we find the figure of
Respublica equating the fluctuations of communal
prosperity with the strengths and weaknesses of
good or bad political leadership: 'Yet by all
experience thus much is well seen, / That in
commonweals while good governors have been /
All thing hath prospered, and where such men do

---

[101] *King John*, <u>Elizabethan History Plays</u>, ed. William A. Armstrong, Oxford,
(1965), p. 187.

lack, / Commonweals decay and all things do go back.'[102]

As mentioned in the above the fox signifies the flattering counsellors at King Richard's court, and the cock of this tale is readily captivated by their flattery: 'Chauntecleer his wynges gan to bete, / As man that koude his traysoun nat espie, / So was he ravysshed with his flaterie.' (*NPT* 3322-24) This is immediately followed by the Nun's Priest's warning to those lords reckless enough to be so tempted: 'Allas, ye lordes, many a fals flatour / Is in youre courtes, and many a losengeour, / That plesen yow wel moore, by my feith, / Than he that sothfastnesse unto yow seith. / Redeth Ecclesiaste of flaterye; / Be war, ye lordes, of hir trecherye.' (*NPT* 3325-30) The significant biblical passage being: 'It is better to hear the rebuke of the wise, than for a man to hear the song of fools.' (*Ecclesiastes*, Chapter 7, verse 5)

Altlhough Professor Hotson was correct to question the fox's changed name from that given in the sources, and he was also right to investigate why this difference occured; however, he failed to question whether such a detail as the naming of the fox 'daun Russel' could simply have resulted from a scribal failure to cross the letter 't' in the word 'russet.' 'Daun Russet' would immediately have

[102] *Respublica*, English Morality Plays and Moral Interludes, Eds. Edgar T. Schell and J. D. Shuchter, New York, (1969).

recalled the russet beast of Chauntecleer's nightmare: 'His colour was bitwixe yelow and reed.' (*NPT* 2902) Chauntecleer 'caste his ye / Among the wortes on a boterflye,' and although full 'war of this fox, that lay ful lowe,' (*NPT* 3373-74) he is shown to accept that the listening to such flattery is 'worth a boterflye.' In Chaucer's source the hens are named '*Pinte ... Bisse et Rousete;*' transferring the name *Rousete* from a yellowish-red hen to a fox of the same colour would present a valid connection to the ongoing tradition; within this tale we have 'Daun Burnel the Asse;' (*NPT* 3312) from 'burnel' or 'burnet' we get 'brown' / O. Fr. *Burnette*.

The Nun's Priest describes his fox to be a 'col-fox;' the original of this 'col' prefix is found six times in the *Roman du Renart* epic: '*parmi le col* / by the neck.'[103] This 'by the neck' is surely what this 'col' of 'col-fox' implies. In the *Roman du Renart*, following his identical response to the fox's flattery, Chanticleer the cock is grabbed by the neck; so is this tale's Chauntecleer when he allows himself to be flattered by his neck-grabbing col-fox: 'The fox stirte up atones, / And by the gargat hente Chauntecleer, / And on his bak toward the wode hym beer.' (*NPT* 3334-36) Within the

---

[103] *How Reynard Caught Chanticleer*, Originals and Analogues, Chaucer Society, F. J. Furnivall, Edmund Brock, and W. A. Coulston, London, (1888), p. 124.

Renard cycle the central character of Renard the fox is often alloted such tags as 'Renard the Red' or 'Renard the plotter of all wickedness;' this 'col-fox' takes on the rather obvious sense of 'Renard the neck grabber.' Contemporary and later usage of *col* also contains this 'neck' connection: '*Concupiscentia carnis* colled me about the nekke'.[104] Two centuries later we find: 'So having sayd, her twixt her armes twine / She streightly strayned, and colled tenderly.'[105]

I believe that Professor Hotson was incorrect when he connected Chauntecleer with Thomas Mowbray the Lord Marshall; and then with two other members of the Mowbray faction. When on such occasions he attempts to make the history agree with his figurative readings of the persons being represented within the allegory he is often drawn into mistaken conclusions: 'But Chaucer is wise enough to let others endite sovereign notabilities ... he is not so stupid to plan a complete allegory of the recent affair. We are not to think that Chaucer intended Chauntecleer to represent Henry Bolingbroke throughout or that there was an original to Pertelote.'[106]

---

[104] *Langland's Piers the Plowman and Richard the Redeless,* ed. Walter Skeat, Vol. 1, Text, Oxford, (1979), p. 611.
[105] *Spenser, Poetical Works,* Book 111, cant II, verse 34. p. 151.
[106]Hotson, (pp. 780-81).

Although the Nun's Priest informs us that his tale is confined to the world of animals: 'My tale is of a cok, as ye may heere, / That tok his conseil of his wyf, with sorwe,' (*NPT* 3252-53) he follows this comment with disparaging remarks on the bad counselling that are often given by womankind: 'Wommennes conseils been ful ofte colde; / Wommannes conseil broghte us first to wo.' (*NPT* 3256-57) He also claims that such sayings are to be taken as being spoken 'in my game;' (*NPT* 3262) but in case this is not acceptable to others amongst the pilgrims, here he is obviously hinting the Wife of Bath; the Prioress and the Second Nun, he also informs us that he is not the author of such an opinion: 'Thise been the cokkes wordes, and nat myne; / I kan noon harm of no womman divyne.' (*NPT* 3265-66)

Probably King Richard / Chauntecleer's fear of his future fate is being expressed in his unease that the nightmare he has experienced foretells his imprisonment and eventual death: '"Now God," quod he, "my swevene recche aright, /And kepe my body out of foul prisoun! / Me mette how that I romed up and doun / Withinne our yeerd, wheer as I saugh a beest / Was lyk an hound, and wolde han maad areest / Upon my body, and wolde han had me deed."' (*NPT* 2896-2901) Following his execution of the Earl of Arundel, in those final tyrannous years he is recorded to have been greatly disquieted by such nightime torments: 'Richard's nights began to be troubled by bad dreams, out of which he would start in terror. He dreamt repeatedly of the earl of Arundel, executed on Tower Hill and buried in the church of the Austin Friars in Broad Street, London. There were stories of miracles at his grave ... Pilgrims began to visit the grave as though the earl was a holy martyr, and when Richard heard the news he fell into one of his recurrent uncontrollable rages, for such a cult could become the seed of revolution. The *Annales* gives a ghoulish account of how he tackled the political problem and tried at the same time to set his mind at rest.'[107]

We should also be mindful of those important changes that take place when Chanticleer and Pinte of the source material become Chaucer's Chauntecleer and Pertelote. In the original Pinte is described to be the best egg layer on Constant Desnoes's farm; Chauntecleer's 'faire damoysele Pertelote' is said to be 'wonder lyk to hym, as of colours,' (*NPT* 2868) and amongst the other hens within his yard she is 'the faireste hewed on hir throte;' (*NPT* 2869) it's clearly Chauntecleer's sexual excitement over Pertelote's beauty that weakens his resolve regarding the warning contained in his prophetic nightmare. Pinte warned the sceptical Chanticleer that his dream implies

[107] Bruce, Marie Louise, pp. 173-74.

danger; Pertelote persuades Chauntecleer to ignore any uneasiness over his 'swevene.' Pinte understood that Chanticleer is the victim of his self-pride and bad behaviour; Pertelote possesses no such awareness. In the *NPT* its Chauntecleer that eventually understands that disaster can occur to the one that 'wynketh whan he sholde see.' (*NPT* 3441)

Alexander Pope's translantion of Homer's *Odyssey* illustrates the danger that such as this tale's sirens / mermaids present to those princes who are foolish enough to heed their seductive melodies: 'O prince attend; some favouring power be kind. / And print the important story on thy mind! / Next, where the Sirens dwell, you plough the seas; / Their song is death, and makes destruction please. / Unblest the man, whom music wins to stay / Nigh the cursed shore, and listen to the lay.'[108] A combination of lustfulness and self-pride: 'Chauntecleer in al his pryde,' (*NPT* 3191) induces the cock down from the beam on the very day he had earlier considered to be threatening to his safety: 'He was namoore aferd. / He fethered Pertelote twenty tyme, / And trad hire eke as ofte, er it was pryme.' (*NPT* 3176-78) King Richard's passionate love for his young queen has been well documented. Recording a contemporary French source, Bevan provides us with his vivid description of the final leave-taking between these

---

[108] Pope, Alexander *The Odyssey of Homer,* The Chandos Classics, London and New York: Frederick Warne and Co. Book XII, p. 167.

two: 'The King took the Queen in his arms and kissed her more than forty times … I never saw so great a lord make so much of, nor show such great affection to a lady as did King Richard to his Queen.'[109]

Chauntecleer's ignoring of the danger posed by the fox takes place on the third day of May: 'Whan that the month in which the world bigan, / That highte March, whan God first maked man, / Was complete, and passed were also, / Syn March (was gon), thritty dayes and two.' (*NPT* 3187-90) This being the very same date as that which King Richard dispensed with the counselling given to him by the appellant lords; and, probably, following this he had once again began to slowly allow those that flattered him back into his court.

Whether or not this is significant I am undecided; however it's recorded that on this same date the ancient Roman festival of the Floralia culminated in an orgy of sexual activity. In their celebration of the *Floralia*, those days associated with fertility and the joys of spring, from April 27 to May 3, the prostitutes of Rome who took these dates to be their own, are recorded to have indulged in excesses of sexual debaucheries on this final day. This date is also described to be highly significant for Chaucer's Pandarus: 'In May, that moder is of

---

[109] Bevan, (p. 142).

monthes glade, / That fresshe floures, blew and white and rede, / Ben quike again, that wynter dede made, / And ful of bawme is fletyng every mede, / When Phebus doth his bryghte bemes sprede / Righte in the white Bole, it so bitidde, / And I shal synge, on Mayes day the thrydde, / That Pandarus, for al his wise speche, / Felt ek his part of loves shotes keene, / That, koude he nevere so wel of loving preche, / It made his hewe a-day ful ofte greene.' (*Tr.* Book II, ll. 50-60)

Not surprisingly, when the col-fox grabs Chauntecleer's neck it's to Venus that the Nun's Priest turns with a plea she should now protect her servant: 'O Venus, that art goddesse of plesaunce, / Syn that thy servant was this Chauntecleer, / And in thy servyce dide al his poweer, / Moore for delit than world to multiplye, / Why woldestow suffre hym on thy day to dye?' (*NPT* 3342-46) Being that King Richard does not appear to have fathered any children, in or out of marriage, there is probably an indicative aside here in the above 'moore for delit than world to multiplye.'

Awareness that Chauntecleer figures King Richard brings a deeper understanding of such passages that have hitherto been given less meaningful interpretations. When we come to understand that the cock stands for Richard's hidden presence we give a very different reading to the belief that the following lines are to be taken as

Chaucer's attack on the poetry of Geoffrey de Vinsauf's *Poetria nova* (c. 1210): 'O Gaufred, deere maister soverayn, / That whan thy worthy kyng Richard was slayn / With shot, compleynedest his deeth so sore, / Why ne hadde I now thy sentence and thy loore, / The Friday for to chide, as diden ye? / For on a Friday, soothly, slayn was he. / Thanne wolde I shewe yow how that I koude pleyne / For Chauntecleres drede and for his peyne.' (*NPT* 3347-54) Then, our awareness of these hidden identities assist us to consider the insertion of the above lines to be drawing a connection between the first poet Geoffrey and the second poet Geoffrey: the first poet Geoffrey's distress on the first King Richard's death being compared here to the second poet Geoffrey's anguish over the impending demise of the second King Richard; that's figured as Chauntecleer the cock.

A greater significance can also be given to such as the tale's Daun Burnel anecdote on the wisdom to treat kindly those we may have earlier considered irrelevant for our future welfare. Had King Richard shown a greater love and respect for his subjects he probably would have retained his 'benefice' when Henry Bolingbroke returned from exile to claim his Lancaster inheritance: 'I have wel rad in Daun Burnel the Asse, / Among his vers, how that ther was a cok, / For that a preestes sone yaf hym a knok / Upon his leg whil he was yong and nyce, / He made hym for to lese his benefice.' (*NPT* 3312-16) Had they been previously been treated with kindness by their sovereign lord, his appreciative subjects probably would then have dutifully 'crowed' in their support of his kingship; indeed, if Henry had not been so badly treated by his kingly cousin, so unjustly robbed of his inheritance and had his period of exile increased to a life-term, it's reasonable to conclude that, as had his father before him, he would have been the very first to powerfully oppose any danger that threatened the safety of the one that was his sovereign and his cousin.

Although Professor Hotson's essay makes interesting reading it also demonstrates the impossibility of successfully grafting an incorrect allegorical reading upon such a large piece of literature as the *Nun's Priest's Tale*. Probably the most noticeable evidence of this come in his attempts to claim Henry's hidden presence behind the figure of the cock: 'Now we have no evidence that Henry of Bolingbroke, like Chauntecleer, was more susceptible to flattery than other men; we do know, however, that if ever riches, accomplishments, and good looks made a man a target for flattery, Henry was that man.'[110] I would consider this differently. Had Professor Hotson

---

[110] Hotson, p. 776.

understood the proud cock to be an allegorical stand-in for King Richard II he would have found ample historical evidence detailing this king's excessive love of flattery; then, it would not have been necessary for him to believe that the cock's identity could be taken or disregarded at his pleasure: 'We are not to think that Chaucer intended Chauntecleer to represent Henry Bolingbroke throughout ... A hit is a hit, and must never be pressed too far.' (ibid. p. 781)

Queen Isabel was seven years old when she first captured King Richard's affections; 'faire damoysele Pertelote' is described to have the 'herte in hold' of Chauntecleer since 'thilke day that she was seven nyght oold.' (*NPT* 2873) Within the tale the exasperated Chauntecleer connects her youthful innocence and that of the seven-year-old King Kenelm: 'His norice hym expowned every deel / His sweven, and bad hym for to kepe hym weel, / For traisoun; but he nas but seven yeer oold.' (*NPT* 3115-17)

Pertelote's real-life identity also appears to be implied in her knowledge of the various humours that 'causeth ful many a man in sleep to crie.' (*NPT* 2934) At this time Queen Isabel's father, Charles VI of France, was Europe's most eminent mental patient, and the unsound state of his mind would probably have greatly disturbed her early childhood: 'In the fit of 1393 the King could not remember who or what he was. He did not know he was King, that he was married, that he had children, or that his name was Charles ... he failed to recognize his children although he knew his brother, uncles, councillors, and servants, and remembered the names of those long dead.'[111] Probably her shame over her father's mental weakness could be the reason why she quickly decides to move away from mention of those 'othere humours'of which she claims familiarity: 'Of othere humours koude I telle also / That werken many a man sleep ful wo: / But I wol passe as lightly as I kan.' (*NPT* 2937-39)

Although we came to our allegorical conclusions from different directions of study; I agree with Professor Hotson's taking the tale's 'mordre wol out' to be an allusion to King Richard's murder of the Duke of Gloucester at Calais in 1399: 'These illustrative anecdotes, as we know, were borrowed from Cicero or Valerius Maximus, and added by Chaucer to the fable. The first and longer of them (which constitutes one-eighth of the entire poem) is a harrowing tale of secret murder, done in a foreign town. Near the end of it, Chaucer digressed from his exemplum original to apostrophize God the just, and to reflect on the discovery of hidden murder. If this emphatic aside,

---

[111] Tuchman, Barbara W, *A Distant Mirror The Calamitous 14th Century*, Penguin Books 1979.(p. 513.)

coupled with the anecdote of the secret murder done in a foreign town, be compared with Gloucester's murder at Calais ... It seems more than possible that Chaucer, in writing the Nun's Priest's Tale, was touching contemporary history.'[112] Professor Hotson was correct in this, it's surely Thomas of Gloucester's voice that we are hearing in the following: 'My gold caused my mordre, sooth to sayn.' (NPT 1321)

Unlike Professor Hotson's more scholarly unease; my sense of this allusion's political significance came from a growing awareness of the *Canterbury Tales* being an ongoing allegory, and from this came my greater conviction of the hidden realities to be found within that same figurative background. Chaucer closes his second of the tale's two main anecdotes with the following: 'O blisful God, that art so just and trewe, / Lo, how that thou biwreyest mordre alway! / Mordre wol out; that se we day by day. / Mordre is so wlatson and abhomynable / To God, that is so just and resonable, / That he wol nat suffre it heled be, / Though it abyde a yeer, or two or thre. / Mordre wol out, this my conclusioun.' (*NPT* 3050 - 57) A few years following Gloucester's murder at Calais in 1397, that unforgivable event was condemned and

---

[112] Hotson, (p. 772).

sternly punished by King Henry IV's in his first parliament.

Although having correctly linked the first of the tale's two main anecdotes with Gloucester's murder at Calais; Professor Hotson failed to consider whether the second anecdote indicated the traditional Ship of State: 'And thus he took his leve, and wente his way. / But er that he hadde half his cours yseyled, / Noot I nat why, ne what myschaunce it eyled, / But casuelly the shippes botme rente, / And ship and man under the water wente.' (*NPT* 3098-3102) Such a symbol of a collapsing state can be found as early as the political lyrics (620-550 B.C.) of Alcaeus:

> I cannot understand how the winds are
> set against each other. Now from this
> side and now from that the waves roll.
> We between them run with the wind
> in our black ship driven, hard pressed
> and labouring under the giant storm.
> All round the mast-step washes the sea
> we shipped. You can see through the
> sail already where there are opening
> rents within it. The forestays slacken....[113]

---

[113] _Greek Lyrics_, Trans. Richard Lattimore, Chicago, (1975), pp. 42-43.

In his summary of the *Canterbury Tales*, the Parson draws a significant connection between personal sin and this allegorical figure of a sinking ship: 'For soothe, synne is in two maneres; outher it is venial or deedly synne. Soothly, whan man loveth any creature more than Jhesu Crist oure Creatour, thanne is it deedly synne. And venial synne is it, if man love Jhesu Crist lasse than hym oghte. / For soothe, the dede of this venial synne is ful perilous, for it amenuseth the love that men sholde han to God moore and moore ... For the proverb seith that "Manye small maken a greet." / And herkne this ensample. A greet wawe of the see comth som tyme with so greet a violence that it drencheth the ship. And the same harm doon som tyme the smale dropes of water, that entren thurgh a litel crevice into the thurrok, and in the botme of the ship, if men be so necligent that they ne discharge hem nat by tyme. / And therefore, although ther be a difference bitwixe thise two causes of drenchynge, algates the ship is dreynt.' (*ParsT* 358-364)

As in the Monk's previous example of Croesus in his tale's closing illustration of a proud and reckless sovereign that lost his power and then suffered the consequences of his earlier folly: 'Ahanged was Cresus, the proude kyng; / His roial trone myghte hym nat availle;' (*MkT* 2759-60) the proud Chauntecleer also decides to ignore his warning nightmare: 'Now let us speke of myrthe,

242

and stynte al this. / Madame Pertelote, so have I blis, / Of o thyng God hath sent me large grace; / For whan I se the beautee of youre face, / Ye been so scarlet reed aboute youre yen, / It maketh al my drede for to dyen; / For al so siker as *In Principio, Mulier est hominis confusio* - / Madame, the sentence of this Latyn is, / Womman is mannes joye and al his blis.' (*NPT* 3157-66)

In their non-figurative reading of this tale, perhaps others have considered that antifeminist humour lies behind the cock's mistaken translation of the above Latin; however, it also happens that up to then Chauntecleer really does consider Pertelote's presence in his life to be the most desirable form of blissful existence; and it's therefore not surprising that he misconstrues the Latin he quotes. It's only later, when he is perched high in the tree at the tale's close that he becomes aware that this form of bliss endangers his physical safety. Frightened, he then he seriously considers the folly of his past behaviour and asks for God's support in his future attempts to replace sensual bliss with spiritual bliss: 'He that wynketh, whan he sholde see, / Al willfully, God lat him nevere thee!' (*NPT* 3426-32)

In this tale the Nun's Priest has contrasted the steadfast future of the Christian with the uncertain safety of those motivated by sensuality and self-pride. Chauntecleer's proud and reckless reign within the widow's yard leads to a life-threatening violence that gives the lie to his original belief of true happiness. Persuaded by sensual passion he has become guilty of loving his 'wyf ... more than resoun requireth,' (*ParsT* 376) and this weakening of his spiritual resolve makes him an easy victim for the flatterers at his court: 'Flaterers been the develes enchauntours; for they make a man to wene of hymself be lyk that he nys nat lyk, / They ben lyk to Judas that bitraysen a man to selle hym to his enemy; that is to the devel.' (*ParsT* 615-16) Being that King Richard had not at that time been dethroned, he remained 'lord' of the country; with Chauntecleer high in the tree it's therefore to his newly understood want of a 'spiritual bliss' that the Nun's Priest alludes in the tale's concluding remark: 'Now, goode God, if that it be thy wille, / As seith my lord, so make us alle goode men, / And brynge us to his heighe blisse! Amen,' (*NPT* 3444-46)

A person of strong religious convictions: 'For oure book seith, Al that is writen is writen for oure doctrine, and that is myn entente;' (*ParsT* 1083) Chaucer closes this allegory with a plea of forgiveness towards the foolish king: 'But ye that holden this tale a folye, / As of a fox, or of a cok and hen, / Taketh the moralite, goode men. / For Seint Paul seith that al that writen is, / To oure doctrine it is ywrite, ywis; / Taketh the fruyt, and lat the chaf be stille.'(*NPT* 3438-43) That is he appears here to be repeating Saint Paul's doctrine of mercy towards all who sincerely repent of their past transgressions; that we should accept that the punishment of those whose actions had previously lacked spiritual discernment should be left to God's better judgment. That we cannot allow ourselves to be motivated by personal feelings of revenge, instead of such we should attempt to follow Christ's example of forgiving those who had subjected his person to the most brutal of hardships and death.

The 'manye places' and the 'many othere places' mentioned in the *Tale of Melibee* are examples of Chaucer's fondness for those biblical tracts that affirm God's grace of mercy to all who sincerely repent their past sins: 'And heerto accordeth Seint Paul the Apostle in manye places. / He seith, Ne yeldeth nat harm for / harm, ne wikked speche for wikked speche, / but do wel to hym that dooth thee harm and blesse hym that seith to thee harm. / And in manye othere places he amonesteth pees and accord.' (*Mel* 1291-94) The political problem being that however sincerely he appeared to have earlier sworn his oaths; Richard simply could not be trusted to keep his word. He may, as he had done with the former appellants, in the future attempt to punish those that had dared to oppose his tyranny.

Perhaps the allegory I have advanced in this reading of Chaucer's beast fable cannot solely be established through the dramatic and humourous interplay of such figures as Chauntecleer; Pertelote and the col-fox. It does however seem to me that if these are taken together with the consistency of the ongoing allegorical history I have presented in this reading; more than likely they are Chaucer's 'fruit' in this tale. An additional reason for my explanations of the tale as an allegory can also be drawn out of such features as Chaucer having adopted the traditional form in the long debate that takes place between Chauntecleer and Pertelote; also in the tale's inclusion of those features that may readily be interpreted as being symbols within this tradition: such as the 'Ship of State' and the 'poor widow.' Possibly the main difficulty others have in acceptance of such carefully placed figures is that the vividness of the pictures Chaucer paints cause them to appear so realistic that they may too readily be accepted in such a manner as allows the *NPT* to be considered as nothing other than a beast fable that closes on a routine moral. Because of this they may become tempted to seek no further explanations of those darker passages I claim to be found within the text.

Professor Hotson described this problem rather well: 'Now the medieval readers did not understand 'art for art's sake;' they preferred useful stories: stories that taught, that satirized, or that pointed an excellent moral. The other poets of the tradition were of the same mind, the attitude of the most 'artistic' of them is declared by Pandarus: "How-so it be that som men hem delyte / With subtil art hir tales for to endyte, / Yet for al that, in hir ententioun, / Hir tale is al for som conclusioun." (*TC* 2. 256-259) Chaucer of course does point us to a moral at the end of this fable, yet I question whether the medieval reader, although delighted with the mock-heroics and pleased with the moral, was satisfied with the very general nature of the satire on human fraility found in the rest of the tale. Moreover, the thing is told with such verve and high spirits, that it is hard not to suspect that author and audience saw something further in it to amuse them: something besides the main comic dialogue, the characters, and the stock situation, which time has hidden from us.'[114]

The Second Nun's Prologue and Tale

This prologue and tale is somewhat problematic regarding its placing within the *Canterbury Tales*. Perhaps the following in the *Complete Works* is the correct assessment: 'The *Second Nun's Prologue and Tale* are held generally,

---

[114] Hotson, pp.763-64.

and with the highest probability, to be early writings of Chaucer, which he took over, but never really adapted, for the *Canterbury Tales*. Even the ascription to the Second Nun appears only in the rubrics, while in the text of the *Prologue* (l. 62) the narrator is referred to as an *unworthy sone of Eve.* Yet there seems no reason for doubting that Chaucer meant to assign the tale to the Nun who attended the Prioress as her *chapeleyne.*[115] Whatever is eventually decided upon by others, I refer the decision of its placing within the series to those that have, or others that probably will in the future add their own more scholarly deliberations on this matter.

Certainly the figures of Valerian, Tiburce and Maximus in the tale suggest three representatives of goodness within King Richard's psyche: 'So in o beynge of divinitee, / Thre persones may ther right wel bee.' (SecNT 340-41) The figure of Almachius communicates the opposite: 'For he Almachius, with ful wikke entente, / To sleen hire.' (SecNT 524-25) Without bringing Queen Isabel into the equation it appears that this tale is closely related to that told by the Prioress. In both tales the innocent figures are described to suffer a similar death: 'This cursed Jew hym hente, and heeld hym faste, / And kitte his throte;' (PrT 571-72) likewise in this tale

---

[115] *The Complete Works*, p.755.

we find: 'Thre strokes in the nekke he smoot hire tho, / The tormentour, but for no maner chaunce / He myghte noght smyte al hir nekke atwo.' (*SNT* 526-528)   The innocence of Cecilie's thoughts at her wedding: 'And whil the organs maden melodie, / To God allone in herte thus sang she: / "O Lord, my soule and eek my body gye / Unwemmed, lest that I confounded be,"' (*SecNT* 134-37) contrasts her eventual mood of spiritual confusion: 'And of thy light my soule in prison lighte, / That troubled is by the contagioun / Of my body, and also by the wighte / Of erthely lust and fals affeccioun; / O havene of refut, O salvacioun / Of hem that been in sorwe and in distresse, / Now help ....' (*SecNT* 71-77)

       When Richard's tyrannical history is reflected upon I find the Second Nun's description of Cecilie's scorn of such power possessed by an Almachius figure appears to be a significant inclusion: 'Youre myght, quod she, ful litel is to dreede, / For every mortal mannes power nys / But lyk a bladdre ful of wynd, ywys. / For with a nedles poynt, whan it is blowe, / May al the boost of it be leyd ful lowe.' (*SecNT* 437-441) Perhaps this was taken up in Shakespeare's presentation of Richard's removal from power:

For within the hollow crown
That rounds the mortal temples of a king
Keeps Death his court, and there the antick
sits,
Scoffing his state and grinning at his pomp;
Allowing him a breath, a little scene,
To monarchize, be fear'd, and kill with looks,
Infusing him with self and vain conceit
As if this flesh which walls about our life
Were brass impregnable; and humoured thus
Comes at the last, and with a little pin
Bores through his castel wall, and farewell
king!
(Richard II, Act III, sc. ii, ll. 160-170).

The Canon's Yeoman's prologue

Being late additions to the pilgrimage these
figures of the Canon and his Yeoman portray King
Richard's growing awareness of the serious
consequences that could now follow his previous
failure to safeguard the right relationship he should
have kept with his subjects: 'His hakeney, that was
al pomely grys, / So swatte that it wonder was to
see; / It semed as he had priked miles three. / The
hors eek that his yeman rood upon / So swatte that
unnethe myghte it gon. / Aboute the peytrel stood
the foom ful hye; / He was of foom al flekked as a
pye.'(*Pro CYT* 559-565) The Canon himself is also

described to be sweating, and seeing this gives the Narrator an emphasised feeling of pleasure: 'He hadde ay priked lik as he were wood. / A clote-leef he hadde under his hood / For swoot and for to keep his heed from heete. / But it was joye for to seen hym swete!'(*Pro 576-579*)

Even this late into the pilgrimage this disposition's love of merriment is stressed: '"God save," quod he, "this joly compaignye! / Faste have I priked, quod he, for youre sake, / By cause that I wolde yow atake, / To riden in this myrie compaignye," / His yeman eek was ful of curteisye, / And seyde, "Sires, now in the morwe-tyde / Out of youre hostelrie I saugh yow ryde, / And warned heer my lord and my soverayan, / Which that to ryden with yow is ful fayn / For his desport; he loveth daliaunce." / "Freend, for thy warnyng God yeve thee good chaunce," / Thanne seyde oure Hoost, "for certain it wolde seme / Thy lord were wys, and so I may wel deme. / He is ful jocund also, dar I leye! / Can he oght telle a myrie tale or tweye, / With which he glade may this compaignye" / "Who, sire? My lord? Ye, ye withouten lye, / He kan of murthe and eek of jolitee / Nat but ynough."' (*Pro CYT 583-601*)

When the Canon leaves the company the prologue's narrative becomes serious, and from that time onwards the Yeoman is left to tell his tale without any threat of interference. What we now find is the Yeoman aspect of King Richard's psyche describing how he has for some time been aware of the trouble this 'merry' canon disposition has caused for him and yet, until this time, it has been difficult for him to gain his freedom from such a frivolous behaviour: 'Syn he is goon, the foule feend hym quelle! / For nevere hereafter wol I with hym meete / For peny ne for pound, I yow beheete, / He that me broghte first unto that game, / Er that he dye, sorwe have he and shame! / For it is ernest to me, by my feith; / That feele I wel, what so any man seith. / And yet, for al my smert and al my grief, / For al my sorwe, labour, and mischief, / I koude nevere leve it in no wise.' (*Pro CYT* 705-714)

The Canon Yeoman's Tale

The tale describes King Richard's failure to repay those debts that his extravagance has amassed: 'I am endetted so therby / Of gold that I have borwed, trewely, / That whil I lyve I shal it quite nevere.' (*CYT 734-36*) Those days the Man of Law had earlier warned against have now come to pass: 'Herkne what is the sentence of the wise: / "Bet is to dyen than have indigence; / Thy selve neighebor wol thee despise. / If thou be povre, farwel thy reverence!" / Yet of the wise man take this sentence: / "Alle the dayes of povre men been wikke. / Be war, therefore, er thou come to that prikke!'" (*MLT* 113-117)

The Yeoman's mention of an earlier period spent at London with a 'wife' rather than with the 'widow' figure suggests that when he was under the wiser counselling of the appellants, King Richard had carried out good services to his subjects and because of these they had tolerated his extravagances: 'In Londoun was a preest, an annueleer, / That therinne dwelled hadde many a yeer, / Which was so plesaunt and so servysable / Unto the wyf, where as he was at table, / That she wolde suffre hym no thyng for to paye / For bord ne clothyng, wente he never so gaye, / And spendyng silver hadde he right ynow.' (*CYT* 1012-18) His behaviour had eventually changed and resulted in actions contradictory to God's desired charity: 'Whoso maketh God his adversarie, / As for to werken any thyng in contrarie / Of his wil, certes, never shal he thryve, / Thogh that he multiplie terme of his lyve.' (*CYT* 1476-79)

The Manciple's Prologue

This tale's prologue commences with the Narrator's: 'Woot ye nat where ther stant a litel toun / Which that ycleped is Bobbe-up-and-doun, / Under the Blee, in Caunterbury Weye?' (*MancPro* 1-3) When the work's allegory is understood we find that there is no good reason to be presenting a little town or a field from the 'Bobbe-up-and-down' description of the Cook's discomfort: 'Probably Harbledown, two miles north of Canterbury on the old road from London, though "Up and down field" in the parish of Thannington and Bobbing, two miles west of Sittingbourne (N&Q 167, 1932m 26), have been suggested.' (*Riverside* p. 952) The implied sense here being that even this late in the pilgrimage the intoxicated King Richard is found to be 'bobbing up and down'on his Horse of State under the 'blee / complexion' of alcohol: 'Thy visage is ful pale.' (*Pro MancT* 30)

In the early *Miller's Prologue* we found an almost identical description of the drunken and pale in colour Miller attempting to keep on his horse: 'The Millere, that for drunken was al pale, / So that unnethe upon his hors he sat.' (Mil Pro 3120-22) So much emphasis is placed on the drunken state of these two pilgrims that the Manciple's prologue appears to be a final comment on King Richard's drunken behaviour: 'Ther gan oure Hooste for to jape and pleye, / And seyde, "Sires, what! Dun is in the myre! / Is ther no man, for preyere ne for hyre, / That wole awake oure felawe al bihynde? / A theef might hym ful lightly robbe and bynde. / See how he nappeth! See how, for cokkes bones, / That he wol falle fro his hors atones!"' (*Pro MancT* 1-10) The Host had earlier named intoxicated Miller as

'Robyn;' and now we find this Cook disposition to be described as 'Bobbe-up-and-doun, / Under the Blee;' that is, under the 'complexion of alcoholic drink,' in 'Caunterbury Weye.'

The above word 'dun,' conveys a 'dusky / dark' colouring; such a description as could be drawing an implied tyrannically connection, as in Chaucer's *Parliament of Fowls*: 'There myghte men the royal egle fynde, / That with his sharpe lok perseth the sonnne, / And othere egles of a lowere kynde, / Of whiche that clerkes wel devyse conne. / Ther was the tiraunt with his fetherews donne / And grey – I mene the goshauk that doth peyne / To bryddes for his outrageous ravyne.' (*Riverside*, pp. 389-90) Apparently 'dunning' was also a term then applied to the behaviour of those that persistently demanded money, the insertion of the word 'dun' into this prologue could therefore present a token of King Richard's tyrannical habit of constantly threatening his subjects for financial assistance. From this it follows that the 'myre / bog' into which this Cook is likely to fall is to be taken as being a figurative description of his financial distress.

The Host's above comment on how easily this drunken pilgrim could be bound and robbed suggests that although this has not as yet taken place, it was likely to be a near event: 'He hath also to do moore than ynough / To kepen hym and his capul out of the slough; / And if he falle from his capul eftsoone, / Thanne shal we alle have ynogh to done / In lifting up his hevy drunken cors.' (Pro MancT 63-67) Such an observation presenting a true warning of that remarkable ease with which Henry Bolingbroke was able to imprison and thereafter 'rob' King Richard of his kingly inheritance.

The Manciple's Tale

This tale divides the meaningful opposites within King Richard's psyche between Phebus 'the semelieste man,' (*MancT* 119) and the 'oon of litel reputacioun;' (*MancT* 253) the wife figures Queen Isabel: 'Now hadde this Phebus in his hous a wyf / Which that he lovede moore than his lyf, / And nyght and day dide evere his diligence / Hir for to plese and doon hire reverence.' (*MancT* 139-42) The tale's crow implies the hidden figure of Chaucer: 'Countrefete the speche of every man / He koude, whan he sholde telle a tale.' (*MancT* 134-35)

The crow expresses its disgust at what it claims to have seen to be taking place between the one 'of litel reputacioun' and the 'she-wolf' wife dispositions. When informing Phebus of this it holds nothing back: 'For al thy waityng, blered is thyn ye / With oon of litel reputacioun, / Noght worth to thee, as in comparisoun, / The montance of a gnat, so moote I thryve! / For on thy bed thy wyf I saugh hym swyve.' (*MancT* 248-52) Phebus' rejection of the crow's truth: 'And to the crowe, O false theef! seyde he, / I wol thee quite anon thy false tale,' (*MancT* 292-93) recalls the Wife of Bath's earlier boast: 'A wys wyf, if that she kan hir good, / Shal beren hym on honde the cow (chough / a crow-like bird) is wood.' (*Pro.WBT* 231-32)

Whereas Phebus, 'the semeliest man' disposition of King Richard had been willing to wait until his wife arrived at her age of puberty before sexual consummation of their marriage; his opposite aspect 'of litel reputacioun' had no such intention. The above mention of 'false theef' could also be highly significant, for it complements the earlier words of the Host to the Manciple: 'But yet, Manciple, in feith thou art to nyce, / Thus openly repreve hym of is vice. / Another day he wole, peraventure, / Reclayme thee and brynge thee to lure; / I meene, he speke wole of smale thynges, / As for to pynchen at thy rekenynges, / That were nat honest, if it cam to preef.'(*Pro MancT* 69-75)

Previously in the *Canterbury Tales* the blame for the implied act of paedophilia has been issued by the various representative figures of King Richard and Queen Isabel; that is by such self-defending aspects as the Shipman or the Wife of Bath. At this near completion of the series Chaucer the Manciple presents his own assessment of responsibility by suggesting that both the 'oon of litel reputacioun' and the 'base of nature she-wolf' have allowed animalistic urges to overcome their human reason: 'But God it woot, ther may no man embrace / As to destreyne a thyng which that nature / Hath natureelly set in a creature.' (*MancT* 160-62)

Perhaps to somewhat lessen the king's blame in this immoral act the wife is compared to a creature of so base a nature that when in heat she takes as her mate: 'The lewedeste wolf that she may fynde, / Or leest of reputacioun.' (*MancT* 184-85) Whatever be the advantages of its cage of gold and the delicacies of a tender diet, the nature of the captive bird is such that it prefers the liberty of the forest 'that is rude and coold' where it 'goon ete wormes and swich wrecchednesse;' (*MancT* 170-71) likewise, although provided with a silken bed, milk and tender meat, the instinct of a cat is such that it will abandon such luxuries in its appetite for a mouse. Here the Manciple is clearly implying that the inability to control such instinctive forces should be confined to the world of animals, to such creatures as those that lack mankind's reasonable human sense and Christian morality.

At this near completion of the series the Manciple's earlier reliance on plain speaking as his guide: 'The wise Plato seith, as ye may rede, / The word moot nede accorde with the dede;' (*MancT* 207-10) appears to be questioned and rejected by a hint of Chaucer's regret at his having been too outspoken in the censure of the one who previously had not only have been his sovereign; but it seems also his friend: 'But nathelees, thus taughte me my dame: "Thyng that is seyd is seyd, and forth it gooth, / Though hym repente, or be hym nevere so looth. / He is his thral to whom that he hath sayd / A tale of which he is now yvele apayd. / My sone, be war, and be noon auctour newe / Of tidynges, wheither they been false or trewe. / Whereso thou come, amonges hye or lowe, / Keep wel thy tonge and thenk upon the crowe."' (*MancT* 354-62).

The Parson's Prologue

A closing summary of how King Richard's reign has lacked moral direction requires such a commendable figure as the Parson to 'knytte up al this feeste and make an ende.' (*ProParsT* 47) From the pilgrimage's commencement: 'Oure Hooste saugh wel that the brighte sonne / The ark of his artificial day hath ronne / The ferthe part, and half an houre and moore, / And though he were nat depe ystert in lore, / He wiste it was the eightetethe day / Of Aprill, that is messager to May;' (*MLT* 1-6) we have now almost arrived at the close of the series: 'The sonne fro the south lyne was descended / So lowe that he nas nat, to my sighte, / Degrees nyne and twenty as in highte.' (*ParsT* 2-4) That is the sun is setting on the figured 'degrees nyne and

259

twenty'of those pilgrims that have here been presented in this 'artistic' description of King Richard / the Host's reign. This is the ending of that portrayed historical 'day;' a day that has here been illustrated to us by means of Chaucer's 'art' as being a pilgrimage between Cheapside and Canterbury Cathedral; not an 'artificial' day in the sense of it being a period between sunrise and sunset.

Reading it without such an allegorical dimension it's not surprising that previous readers have found this closing prologue's mention of the moon's exaltation in Libra to be troublesome: 'Therwith the moones exaltacioun - / I meene Libra - alwey gan ascende / As we were entryng at a thropes ende.' (*ParsT* 10-12) 'Skeat suggests Chaucer confused "exaltation" with "face" ... Wood argues that Chaucer mentions Libra for a symbolic allusion to divine justice.' (Riverside, p. 955) Elsewhere we find: 'Tyrwhitt suggests that "the mones" is an error for "Saturnes." In support of this most probable explanation may be adduced an article in the Athenaeum of May, 1902, by R. Garnett, in which he wrote: "It is impossible that Chaucer should have been in error on such a subject. The difficulty probably arises from 'Saturn' having been expressed in the archetypal MS. by its astronomical symbol, which was mistaken for the symbol of the moon. Both are curved in shape, the one denoting the lunar crescent, the other the crooked pruning-knife emblematic of Saturn. The handle of the latter is represented by a perpendicular stroke. If this were omitted, or indistinctly delineated, the symbols might easily be confused.""[116]

I believe that only an acceptance of the *Canterbury Tales* as being an allegorical portrayal of King Richard II's reign can overcome such a difficulty; then, with our connection of the work to King Richard's history, the above mentioned Libra becomes meaningful: King Richard / the Host's reign ended on Michaelmas Day, September 29, 1399, and at that time the moon's presence ascends in Libra from September 29 to October 20. Probably this is the correct historical pointer that Chaucer sought to convey. September 29th being the date of King Richard's dethronement. 'Alwey gan' / progressively begins, being a fairly positive pointer to this astrological dating.

The above 'thropes ende' I take to be another of Chaucer's compound words: 'thro' / to overthrow; 'pes' / peace, probably this word was created to indicate that Richard's oppression had been 'overthrown' and that 'peace' will thereafter follow. An anonymous contemporary political poem is titled *Truthe, Reste, and Pes*, and it

---

[116] Wyatt, A.J., The Links Of The Canterbury Tales, Sidgwick & Jackson, London, (1935) p. 105.

expresses identical sentiments to the above: 'And ende of batayle bygynneth pes.'(l. 88)[117] 'Thro,' not the now accepted 'thorp' / village; surely this was Chaucer's intention in his use of the word: 'No village is known to have existed between Harbledown and Canterbury.' (*Riverside*, p. 955).

Historically, the twenty-nine pilgrims that have been figured as being various degrees, dispositions, or aspects of Chaucer; of King Richard and of Queen Isabel's personalities, are now less significant and the passing of their pilgrimage through life can therefore be justly marked by such a corresponding ending of the allegorically described eclipse of the Host's reign. The setting sun becoming a fitting symbolic backdrop of this: 'Fulfilled is my sentence and my decree; / I trowe that we han herd of ech degree; / Almoost fulfild is al myn ordinaunce.' (*ParsT* 17-19) 'Sentence,' 'decree' and 'ordinaunce,' these being words that were readily associated with kingly authority. Tyrwhitt informed us that the phrase: 'Oure Hoost hadde the wordes for us alle,' (*ParsT* 67) were words that specifically expressed governmental control.[118]

The Parson disposition of Chaucer rejects 'fables and swich wrecchednesse / Why sholde I

---

[117] The poem *Truthe, Reste, and Pes*. See TEAMS Texts.

[118] Tyrwhitt, (Speaker of the Commons in Rot. Parl. 51 E III, n. 87.

sowen draf out of my fest, / Whan I may sowen whete, if that me lest?' (*ParsT* 34-6). This changed form of this next tale's presentation signifies the failure of his previous allegorical counselling and the hoped for success of what will be a directly expressed subject matter. Such a directness of presentation as is described by Christ in Saint John's Gospel: 'These things have I spoken unto you in proverbs: but the time cometh, when I shall no more speak unto you in proverbs, but I shall shew you plainly of the Father;' (Saint John's Gospel, Chapter 16, verse 25) again: "His disciples said unto him, Lo, now speakest thou plainly, and speakest no proverb."' (ibid., verse 29)

Even the Host is now ready to listen to the Parson's summary: 'Oure Hoost hadde the wordes for us alle; / "Sire preest," quod he, "now faire yow befalle! / Telleth," quod he, "youre meditacioun. / But hasteth yow; the sonne wole adoun: / Beth fructuous, and that in litel space, / And to do wel God sende yow his grace! / Say what yow list, and we wol gladly heere." / And with that word he seyde in this manere.' (*Pro ParsT* 67-74)

The Parson's Tale

With a constant repeat of the Bible's promise that a sinner 'may arise thurgh penitence;' (*ParsT* 91) the Parson commences his telling of the old sentences: 'Manye been the weyes espirituels that leden folk to our Lord Jhesu Crist and to the regne of glorie. / Of whiche weyes ther is a ful noble wey and a ful convenable, which may nat fayle to man ne to woman that thurgh synne hath mysgoon fro the righte wey of Jerusalem celestial / and this wey is cleped Penitence ... Seint Ambrose seith that Penitence is the pleynynge of man for the gilt that he hath doon, and namoore to do any thing for which hym oghte to pleyne ... But nathelees, men shal hope that every tyme that man falleth, be it never so ofte, that he may arise thurgh Penitence, if he have grace; but certeinly it is greet dout. / For, as seith Seint Gregorie, "Unnethe ariseth he out of his synne that is charged with the charge of yvel usage." / And therefore repenant folk, that stynt for to synne and forlete synne er that synne forlete hem, hooly chirche holdeth hem siker of hire savacioun. / And he that synneth and verraily repenteth hym in his laste, hooly chirche yet hopeth his savacioun, by the grete mercy of oure Lord Jhesu Crist, for his repentaunce; but taak the siker wey.' (*ParsT* 79-94)

Most of the sins listed in this tale can be applied to the whole of humanity: 'Therfore, al the while that a man hath in hym the peyne of concupiscence, it is impossible but he be tempted somtime and moeved in his flesh to synne. / And this thing may nat faille as longe as he lyveth;' (*ParsT* 339-40) however, there remain certain evils which appear to be specific pointers to the passing reign. For example, the *CT*'s constant theme of King Richard's historically recorded dotage love towards his child bride could be implied in the sin of loving 'wyf or child, or oother worldly thing, moore than resoun requireth.' (*ParsT* 376) King Richard's extravagant wardrobe could be suggested in 'the first synne, that is in superfluitee of clothynge, which that maketh it so deere, to harm of the peple.' (*ParsT* 416) His large bodyguard of the brutal and hated Cheshire archers being condemned in the 'holdynge of greet meyneee, whan they be of litel profit or of right no profit, / and namely whan that meynee is felonous and damageous to the peple by hardynesse of heigh lordshipe or by wey of offices. / For certes, swiche lords sellen thanne hir lordshipe to the devel of helle, whanne they sustenen the wikkednesse of hir meynee.' (*ParsT* 436-38)

The lavish feasts within the royal palaces appear in the Parson's condemnation of prodigality at the table: 'In excesse of diverse metes and drynkes, and namely swich manere bake-metes and dish-metes, brennynge of wilde fir and peynted and castelled with papir, and semblabe wast, so that it is abusioun for to thynke.' (*ParsT* 445) King Richard's revengeful murder of the Duke of Gloucester and Richard of Arundel appear to be be implied in the following: 'Right as a justice dampneth hym that is coupable to the deeth. But lat the justice be war that he do it rightfully, and that he do it nat for delit to spille blood but for kepynge of rightwisnesse.' (*ParsT* 571)

Occasionally we detect condemnations that imply connections to specific tales. Such as the linking of a gluttonous disposition with the later appearance of the lecher: 'After Glotonye thane comth Lecherie, for thise two synnes been so ny cosyns that ofte tyme they wol nat departe;' (*ParsT* 836) that is, such a change of personality as is evidenced in 'the strange knight's' appearance after the specified third course of the *Squire's Tale*. Contradiction of January's words: 'A man may do no synne with his wyf, / Ne hurte hymselven with his owene knyf;' (*MerT* 1839-40) is apparent in the following: 'And for that many man weneth that he may nat synne for no likerousnesse that he dooth with his wyf, certes, that opinion is fals. God woot, a man may sleen himself with his owene knyf.' (*ParsT* 859).

Queen Isabel's mastery over her husband and the social consequences that accompanies this attainment appears to be implied in the following: 'Now comth how that a man sholde bere hym with his wif, and namely in two thynges; that is to seyn, in suffraunce and reverence, as shewed Crist whan he made first woman. / For he ne made hire nat of the heved of Adam, for she sholde nat clayme to greet lordshipe. / For ther as the woman hath the maistrie, she maketh to muche desray. Ther neden none ensamples of this; the experience of day by day oghte suffise.' (*ParsT* 925-27)

Conclusion

If this had not been Chaucer's intention I believe it would be impossible to superimpose as consistent an allegorical reading of such length as I have presented above in this reading of the *Canterbury Tales*. However, in a further attempt to confirm the truth of my explanations of these tales having an allegorical dimension, I will now demonstrate how such a figurative reading of King Richard's II's reign is equally valid when it's applied to Chaucer's shorter lyrics.

Titled *Scogan*, the following short poem would have been composed in late 1399 or early 1400; and it implies Chaucer's attempt to share and thereby lessen Richard's grief over the loss of his kingly power. In it he is rebuked for the offence of having renounced his throne and is also counselled to seek God's forgiveness for his past misdeeds.

Scogan

Tobroken been the stautz hye in hevene
That creat were enternally to dure,
Syth that I see the bryghtes goddis sevene
Mowe wepe and wayle, and passion endure.
As may in erthe a mortal creature.
Allas, from whennes may thys thing procede,
Of which errour I deye almost for drede?

By word eterne whilom was yshape
That fro the fyfthe sercle, in no manere,
Ne myghte a drope of teeres doun escape.
But now so wepith Venus in hir spere
That with hir teeres she wol drenche us here.
Allas! Scogan, this is for thyn offence;
Thow causest this diluge of pestilence.

Hastow not seyd, in blaspheme of the goddis,
Thrugh pride, or through thy grete rekelnesse,
Swich thing as in the lawe of love forbode is,
That, for thy lady sawgh nat thy distresse,
Therefore thow yave hir up at Michelmesse?
Allas! Scogan, of olde folk ne yong
Was never erst Scogan blamed for his tongue.

Thow drowe in skorn Cupide eke to record
Of thilke rebel word that thou has spoken,
For which he wol ne lenger be thy lord.
And, Scogan, though his bowe be nat broken,
He wol nat with his arwes been ywroken
On the, ne me, ne noon of oure figure;
We shul of him have neyther hurt ne cure.

Now, certes, frend, I dreede of thy unhap,
Lest for thy gilt the wreche of Love precede
On alle hem that ben hoore and rounde of
shap.
That be so lykly folk in love to spede,
Than shal we for oure labour han no mede;
But wel I wot, thow wolt answere and saye;
'Lo, olde Grisel lyst to ryme and playe!'

Nay Scogan, say not so, for I m'excuse –
God help me so! – in no rym, dowteles,
Ne think I never of slep to wake my muse,
That rusteth in my shethe stille in pees.
While I was yong, I put hir forth in prees;
But al shal passe that men prose or ryme;
Take every man hys turn, as for his tyme.

Envoy

Scogan, that knelest at the stremes hed
Of Grace, of alle honour and worthynesse,
In th'ende of which strem I am dul as ded,
Forgete in solytarie wildernesse, -
Yet, Scogan, thence on Tullius kyndenesse;
Mynne thy frend, there it may fructyfye!
Far-wel, and loke thow never eft Love
dyffye.
(*Riverside*, p. 655)

A belief that the intended recipient of this poem possessed the surname Scogan appears to have confused previous critics in their interpretation of its content: 'The reference to a diluge of pestilence (l. 14) caused by Scogan's renounciation of Love at Michaelmas led Skeat to date the poem in late 1393, because of the recorded floods around Michaelmas in that year. There were, however, other seasons of heavy rain (Brusendorff, Ch Trad. 219, suggests July and August 1391, and Fisher notes rains and floods in March 1390), and determining a precise date is impossible.' (*Riverside*, p. 1086)

Instead of the above readings I believe that the poem contains a hidden dimension of King Richard's reckless behaviour as sovereign; and that a pseudonym reflecting this attitude has been inserted by means of the name Scogan. If this matter of the name is not relevant it seems rather strange that it has been so often (seven times) inserted into such a short poem. Probably Tyrwhitt provided an important clue when he claimed its generic connotations of jester or buffoon.[119] Following from this I came to believe this 'Sco / gan' to be another of Chaucer's compound words; the two parts here being 'sco' as in the poem's mention of scorn and scoff; 'gan,' being the Middle

---

[119] Tyrwhitt, *The Poetical Works of Geoffrey Chaucer*,(p. 449).

English word for 'did;' such as is found in 'gan for the soules preye.' (*GP* 301) By means of his reckless scoffing and scorning of the kingly role, Richard / Scogan 'gan' / *sco*rned and *sco*ffed his royalty; and because of this he eventually ended up having to relinquish the throne.

With this abdication Richard would also have forfeited that considerable temporal power he had previously possessed in such matters as securing mistresses for himself at his royal court. Because of this present inability he could justifiably be described as having also scorned his Lady Venus when she is accompanied by Cupid her servant: 'Thow drowe in skorn Cupide eke.' (l.22) Chaucer attempts to humour Richard's anguish with the jest that such action could result in others, such as Chaucer himself, those who are 'hoor and rounde of shap / That ben so lykly folk in love to spede,' (ll. 31-2) also being made to suffer in the goddess's forthcoming wrath against mankind.

Clearly, this poem cannot be given a successful reading without a prior understanding of the opposites that constitute the 'lawe of love' (l. 17) and the 'wreche of Love.' (l. 30) The 'law of love' indicated the traditionally recognised divine measure of kindly actions within the cosmic setting of God's ordained universal order: 'The sun, the king, primogeniture hang together;'[120] the 'wretch of love' representing an excessive love of self-directed love.

Scogan's breaking of the statutes 'that creat were enternally to dure,' (l. 2) are linked to: 'Thilke rebel word that thou has spoken.' (l.23) By this Chaucer appears to be indicating King Richard's renounciation of his throne with its fixed feudal system of loyalty and feudal degrees; the 'lawe of love' that the sovereign's role was established to maintain and protect until his death. This 'errour' and the dread of its future consequences being such as fills Chaucer with foreboding: 'I deye almost for drede.' (l. 7) The poem's indication that 'Thou yave hir up at Michelmesse,' (l. 19) alluding to King Richard's renounciation of his throne on Michaelmas Day, September 29, 1399.

Richard's insistence on reading aloud the abdication schedule was considered to be so unusual an event that mention of it could certainly have been inserted into a contemporary poem of the recent affair: 'Be it remembered that on Monday, the feast of St. Michael, in the 23rd year of the reign of King Richard II … he said openly before them that he was ready to make renunciation and resignation … and although, to avoid the labour of such lengthy reading, he might, as he was told, have

---

[120]Tillyard, E.M.W., The Elizabethan World Picture, Penguin Books,1970, (p. 18).

read the renunciation … by deputy, the King, holding the schedule in his hand said at once willingly, as it seemed, and with cheerful looks, that he would read it himself. And he read it through distinctly, absolving his lieges, and making renunciation, oath, and declaration as is fully contained in the said schedule.'[121] This description certainly agrees with Chaucer's overall portrayal of King Richard's 'merry' disposition within the above allegories.

This poem's first five verses depict the social fall of one whose behaviour had maintained the sensual rule of Venus: 'Festes, instrumentz, caroles, daunces, / Lust and array, and alle the circumstaunces / Of love.' (*KnT* 1931-33) Although this light-heartedness of tone is retained into the fifth verse, there follows from there onwards an expression of concern over Scogan's present misery: 'Now, certes, freend, I drede of thy unhap;' and this foreboding sets the mood of what follows. This verse's conclusion: 'But wel I wot, thow wolt answere and saye; / "Lo, olde Grisel lyst to ryme and playe."' (ll. 34-5) The above suggests a one-time friendship of verse and laughter that had at an earlier period existed between the former king and his poet.

---

[121] Hughes, pp. 286-289.

The sixth verse, in which Chaucer seeks God's assistance in his resolve to turn away from such as he now considers to have been his foolishly expressed past poetical endeavours: 'For I m'excuse - / God help me so,' (ll. 36-7) indicates the uncertainty of the changed times. Having formerly dedicated so much of his literature to King Richard's moral instruction, and of late witnessed the political ruin and physical danger that faced his one-time pupil, Chaucer's mood becomes grim as he considers the passing of his failed service: 'But al shal passe that men prose or ryme; / Take every man hys turn, as for his tyme.' (ll. 41-2)

The poem's Envoy displays an understanding of how the former king's need of support has now become something very different to that he previously required. Richard's unlawful and cruel acts against the interests of his subjects must now be atoned by his kneeling 'at the stremes hed / Of Grace.' (ll. 43-4) Chaucer's previous attempts to instruct his king in moral behaviour placing him 'of alle honour and worthynesse, / In th'ende of which strem.' (ll. 44-5) Disregarding Richard's later neglect of his former friend: 'forgete in solytarie wildernesse,' Chaucer nevertheless promises to plead on his behalf.

As the opportunity to influence Richard's behaviour into good government was now passed, this poem's mention of Tullius / Cicero's kindness probably alludes to the first of the following two instances of friendship that Richard would have found in his copy of the *Romance of the Rose*:

> Except only in causes two:
> If men his freend to deth wold drive,
> Lat hym be bisy to save his lyve;
> Also if men wolen hym assayle,
> Of his wurshipp to make hym faile,
> And hyndren hym of his renoun,
> Lat hym, with full entencioun,
> His dever don in ech degre
> That his freend ne shamed be
> (*Rom* 5292-5300)

In the above Cicero referred to political problems: 'If someone in public life gets into difficulties, people find it deeply disagreeable and painful to remain friends with him; and those who are prepared to join him in his trouble are very few indeed. As Ennius rightly said, a friend in need is a friend indeed. There are two opposite charges on which men stand convicted of fickleness and unreliability. When they are doing well, and when a friend is in difficulties they desert him.'[122]

---

[122] Cicero, <u>On the Good Life</u>, Penguin Classics, (1971), p. 209.

Having throughout the reign considered himself to have been a true friend of his former king; Chaucer cannot now allow the final opportunity of interceding on Richard's behalf to pass without attempting to explain, and thereby to somewhat lessen his guilt. This poem therefore closes on a declaration of his continued friendship, and with this comes an implied promise to 'fructyfye' on Scogan's behalf: 'Mynne thy frend, there it may fructyfye! / Far-wel, and loke thow never eft Love dyffye.' (ll. 48-9) Obviously charitable love is that form of love being alluded to in these lines.

I take the following short poem that's now titled 'Bukton' to be Chaucer's defence of his former king and friend. Apparently the 'Bukton' heading is absent in the earliest edition of the poem. Professor Skeat gave the following observations as to its dating and contents: 'This piece is certainly genuine. In MS, F., the title is - 'Lenvoy de Chaucer a Bukton.' In Julian Notary's edition it is - 'Here foloweth the counceyll of Chaucer touching Maryag, &c. Whiche was sente to (sic) Bucketon, &c.' In all the other early printed editions it is inserted without any title ... The Poem is one of Chaucer's latest productions, and may safely be dated about the end of the year 1396. This appears from the reference, in l. 23, to the great misfortune it would be to any Englishmen 'to be take in Fryse,' i.e. to be taken prisoner in Friesland ... The expedition set out in August, 1396, and stayed in Friesland about five weeks, till the beginning of October, when 'the weather began to be very cold and to rain almost daily.' The great danger of being taken prisoner in Friesland was because the Frieslanders fought so despearately that they were seldom taken prisoners themselves. Then the Frieslandes offered their prisoners in exchange, a man for man; but, when their enemies had none to give in return, they put them to death. Beside this, the prisoners had to endure all the miseries of a bad and cold season, in an inclement climate. Hence the propriety of Chaucer's allusion fully appears.'[123]

I take this poem to have been written three or more years later than the above mentioned 1396; sometime following Richard's 1399 imprisonment; and definitely before John Holland's attempted rescue of him in 1400. Most likely the 'Bukton' inclusion came about with awareness that a Lancastrian partisan surnamed Bukton had become responsible for the former king's custody. Whatever the reason behind the poem's original omission of a title, its figurative message implies that it was eventually intended to be passed onwards as a personal plea from Chaucer to King Henry IV:

[123] Skeat, Walter, W., *Chaucer the Minor Poems*, Oxford, At The Clarendon Press, M DCCC LXXVIII. (pp.lxxviii – lxxix)

Bukton

My maister ..., whan of Crist our kyng
Was axed what is trouthe or sothfastnesse,
He nat a word answered to that axing,
As who saith, 'No man is al true,' I gesse.
And therefore, though I highte to expresse
The sorwe and wo that is in marriage,
I dar not written of it no wikkednesse,
Lest I myself fall eft in swich dotage.

I wol nat seyn how that yt is the cheyne
Of Sathanas, on which he gnaweth evere;
But I dar seyn, were he out of his peyne,
As by his wille he wolde be bounde nevere.
But thilke doted fool that eft hath levere
Ycheyned be than out of prison crepe,
God let him never fro his wo dissevere,
Ne no man him bewayle, though he wepe!

But yet, lest thow do worse, take a wyf;
Bet ys to wedde than brenne in worse wise.
But thow shal have sorwe on thy flesh, thy
lyf,
And ben thy wives thrall, as seyn these wise;
And yf that hooly writ may nat suffyse,
Experience shal the teche, so may happe,
That the were lever to be taken in Frise
Than eft to fall of weddyng in the trappe.

Envoy

This lytel writ, proverbs, or figure
I sende yow, take kepe of yt, I rede;
Unwys is he that kan no wele endure.
If thow be siker, put the nat in drede'.
The Wyf of Bathe I pray yow that ye rede
Of this matere than we have on honed.
God graunte yow your lyf freely to lede
In fredam; for ful hard is to be bonde.
(Riverside, pp. 655-56)

When taken together with our knowledge of the former king's history, and also of the allegorically format of the *Canterbury Tales*, this 'Bukton' poem can certainly be considered of historical importance. Notice here how the likely closeness of King Henry's accession to the throne determines an immediate and respectful indication of Chaucer's loyalty: 'My maister ..., whan of Crist our kyng,' (1.1) and it would also have been impossible to improve on the poem's opening statement in the former king's defence. That is, King Henry is reminded how the greatest of moral authorites: 'Crist is verray trouthe,' (ParsT 593) had remained silent in answer to the question of 'what is trouthe or sothfastnesse' (1. 2) in human behaviour; such a silence implying that 'no man is al trewe, I gesse.' (1.4)

The poem's 'and therefore' (l. 5) suggests that 'thilke doted fool' (l. 13) had behaved in such a way as he did due to the 'sorwe and wo that's to be found in marriage' when the husband dotes on his wife. Mention here of the Wife of Bath is therefore of crucial important to our understanding of the poem. King Henry is requested to consider how Queen Isabel / the Wife of Bath had influenced her infatuated husband into a total acceptance of her rule: 'The Wyf of Bathe I pray yow that ye rede / Of this matere than we have on honed.' (ll. 29-30) Although the poem does not question the correctness of the institution of marriage; it certainly condemns that marital state in which sensual passion enslaves a man to the rule of his wife: 'I would ne lenger in the bed abyde, / If that I felte his arm over my side, / Til he had maad his raunson unto me; / Than wold I suffer hym to do his nycetee' (*WBT* 409-12).

Chaucer turns away from what he considers to have been the main cause of Richard's reckless behaviour and issues a plea for his present miserable situation. Should King Henry now consider himself to be secure on his throne: 'If thow be siker, put the nat in drede;' (l. 28) perhaps the former king's freedom could even enhance the common good: 'Unwys is he that kan no wele endure.' (l. 27) The final words in this matter implying a comparison between King Henry's own liberty and the pitiful state of Richard's captivity: 'God graunte yow your lyf freely to lede / In fredam; for ful hard is to be bonde' (ll. 31-2). Undoubtedly John Holland's assassination attempt of King Henry and his family; and following from this his planning to reinstate Richard on the throne, would have ended any hope of the former king's redemption. Probably it was this failed undertaking that necessitated Richard's death in captivity.

Appendix

I have decided to provide this short explanation of what happened leading up to and following King Richard's abdication and death; that is to disclose the later history experienced by the three main personalities explored by Chaucer within the above *Canterbury Tales*. However brief this review leading us up to the time of their deaths; perhaps that little extra knowledge of this account can be considered interesting.

King Richard's final short spell of life following his abdication was as miserable as it possible could have been for one who had previously possessed all the bounties of nature and the material advantages that a person could desire: 'News was brought to the Duke that Richard of Bordeaux was asking for him and greatly desired to speak to him. He immediately left his palace – it was late afternoon – and went by barge down the Thames, accompanied by his knights. He entered the Tower by the back way and went into the keep where the King was. Richard greeted him with great courtesy, making himself very humble before him, like the frightend man he was, and said: "Cousin, I have been thinking over my position, and God knows it is weak enough! I see that I should no longer think of wearing a crown and ruling a nation. If God would receive my soul, I could wish I were out of this life by a natural death and that the King of France should have his daughter back, for we have not had much pleasure together; nor, since I brought her to England, have I ever been on the same good terms with my people as before. Having considered it carefully, cousin, I fully see and admit that I have behaved very wrongly towards you and several nobles of my own blood in this country, and I realize that such things have made peace and forgiveness impossible for me. Therefore, I gladly and willingly resign to you the crown of England, and I beg you to accept it as a freely offered gift."

On hearing this, the Duke of Lancaster answered: "What you have said makes it necessary to assemble representatives of the three estates of England. Indeed, I have already written to summon the prelates and nobles of the country and the Councillors of the principal towns. Within three days there will be enough of them here for you to make the resignation which you desire in due form ... Because my uncle of Gloucester and the Earl of Arundel wisely and loyally remonstrated with you and tried to preserve the honour and achievements of their fathers, you treacherously had them killed. For my part, I have taken you under my protection and I will defend you and prolong your life, through human pity, as far as I can. I will plead your cause before the Londoners and the heirs of those whom you unjustly put to death.' "My deepest thanks," said the King. "I have more trust in you than in all the rest of England." "Rightly," said the Duke. "If I did not go – and had not already gone – against the will of the people, you would have been their prisoner and deposed amid humiliation and mockery, and put to death as your evil deeds deserve." King Richard swallowed all these things which the Duke of Lancaster said to him and had nothing to say in reply. He quite saw that neither force nor argument could help him, but only meekness, friendliness and plain dealing. He made himself as humble as he could, continually begging the Duke of Lancaster that his life should be spared.'[124]

The problem King Henry faced being that Richard had in the past constantly shown himself to be incapable of keeping such oaths; even those that he had previously sworn to uphold with the greatest of solemnity. However sincerely these appeared to have been given, he could not be trusted in the granting of his promises of forgiveness. Froissart adds the following: 'It was said to the King: "Sire, as long as Richard of Bordeaux is alive, neither you nor the country will be secure." The King replied: "I think you are right. But for my part I will never put him to death, since I took him under my

---

[124] *Froissart: Chronicles.* (pp. 459- 461) Selected and Translated and Edited by Geoffrey Brereton, Penguin Books, 1968.

protection. I will keep my promise to him until it becomes apparent that he is behaving treasonably."

The King's knights said: "It would be better for you if he were dead rather than alive. As long as the French know that he is there they will want to make war on you. They will hope to restore him to the throne, because he is married to the King of France's daughter." To this the King of England made no reply, but went out of the room and left them talking together. He went to see his falconers and, placing a falcon on his wrist, became absorbed in feeding it.

Not many days afterwards a true report ran through London that Richard of Bordeaux was dead. From what cause and how it happened I did not know at the time when I wrote these chronicles ... Now, lords, consider well, kings, dukes, counts, prelates, all men of noble lineage and power, how fickle are the chances of this world. King Richard reigned over England for twenty-two years in great prosperity, holding rich estates and fiefs. No King of England before had come within a hundred thousand florins a year of spending as much as he did on the mere upkeep of his court and the pomp that went with it.' (ibid. pp. 468 -469)

Surely not so much the fickleness of fortune as Froissart appears to suggest; King Richard's downfall came about as Chaucer constantly implied it would; in no small part his fall was 'necessitated' by the reckless behaviour to be found in the actions of this proud lord that disdained the good of his subjects in order to glory himself in such matters as the above described 'mere upkeep of his court and the pomp that went with it.'

Queen Isabel's time leading up to her death can also be considered to have been as grim, if not even more harrowing than that of her husband. It is believed that for a time King Henry IV refused to allow her return to France; but her firm refusal to marry his eldest son eventually resulted in his yielding in the matter and following from this she was shipped back into the custody of her father's court.

On 29 June 1406, a time shortly before she arrived at her seventeenth year, Isabel was again married off: this time to her cousin Charles, Duke of Orleans. Her husband being five years her junior, the marriage was presumed not to have been sexually consummated until some three years later; soon after this Isabel became pregnant and is recorded to have died aged 22 on the day following her daughter's birth. Clearly this young queen had experienced a very sad life from a commenced in the company of an often frantically insane father; then through her traumatic experiences in England, and finally the above horror of her ill-fated death on the birth of her daughter.

I believe that Dr. Thomas Gascoigne's report of Chaucer's deathbed lamentation over those works in which he 'portrayed the evil love of men for women' could be taken as being true. If the known historical Thomas Chaucer was Geoffrey Chaucer's son, as it's now claimed in the Life-Records,[125] it seems that Dr. Gascoigne had gained this information through a personal acquaintance.

The *Chaucer Life Records* edition seems to have very carefully mapped out the most likely date of Chaucer's death: 'The traditional date of Chaucer's death is 25 October 1400. The lack of any evidence of the Michaelmas or later payment upon his annuities supports this date ... The date 25 October 1400, as that of Chaucer's death, rests upon the now illegible inscription placed upon the tomb, which, according to John Stow, was erected by Nicholas Bringham in Westminster Abbey in 1556. The inscription was published in 1606. Stow states that Chaucer was buried in Westminster Abbey in the year 1400.'[126]

---

[125] Crow and Olson, p. 543.
[126] Ibid. p. 548)

288

Index

Abbreggynge = to diminish
Almageste = Ptolemy's treatise of astrology.
Ambes as = double aces
Amonesteth = admonish
Arête = blame me. Impute.
Areysen = to be raised
Assage = siege
Assoilen = absolve
Atazir = evil influence.
Augrym stones = counters for an abacus.
Avysioun = prophetic warning.
Bailly = manager of an estate.
Bar = bare / uncover
Bismotred with his habergeon = stained by his coat of mail.
Boose of a bokeler = a raised centre of a shield
Boote = boot / remedy.
Browet = broth
Bythought = on account of a thought
Catel = possessions
Cherl = an oafish person
Chyvachie = military campaigns.
Chevyssaunce = financial borrowings
Contek = strife
Crokk = pot

Deere ynogh a jane = a halfpenny / worthless.
Deslavee = foul
Delve = dig
Demeth = is judged
Devoir = duty.
Devys = opinion.
Digne = worthy of respect.
Doctrine = instruction
Doom = decision
Dyke = ditches
Endyte = write
Erst = first time.
Eyled = ailed
Farsed = stuffed.
Fayn = glad
Fetisly = elegant
Filet = head band
Filthele = fiddle.
Floytynge = flute playing.
Forpyned = wasted away
Fructify = Lat. *Fructus* = fruit. / bearing fruit / to fruition.
Fustian = coarse clooth.
Gise = guide
Gleedes = embers / live coal.
Gree = graciously.
Gypon = tunic.
Haryed = plunder.
Haunchebones = thighs.

Haunt = usual abode
Hertis = heart
Hy sentence = good comments.
Hyndis = service
Hazard = gambling.
Infect = invalid
Kithe = show jealousy
Lede = guide
Letuaries = remedies
Lemman = my love.
Lever = rather
Maugree hir heed = against her will.
Mendemants = summonses.
Mead = meadow.
Misericorde = mercy
Myte = a small Flemish coin of little value.
Nonys = nuns, or on this occasion
Nye = bare of money as a friar's tonsure.
Nyghtertale = nightime.
Parfay = by my faith.
Parvys = church porch used to settle accounts
Payndemayn = very white bread
Perree = precious stones.
Penaunce = penance
Pissmyre = an ant
Priketh = piercing stroke
Prohemye = prologue
Psaltry = harp like instrument.
Pynche = find a flaw.

Pynnes = broaches.
Queynt = extinguished
Raft = taken by force
Reed = counsel
Regne = kingdom
Rekkith = cares
Rewe = have pity
Sautrie = a sort of harp
Seintuarie = sanctuary
Semblable = similar
Sentence = meaning
Sheeldes = French crown coins
Shente destroyed
Snybben = rebuke.
Sondry = various
Sterve = die of famine
Stepe = bright / glittering
Stot = term of abuse / horse
Span = seven to nine inches.
Susteen = endure
Sweven = dream.
Sys cynk = losing throw
Taillynges = taxes
Tholed = suffered
Trowe = believe.
Typet = dangling tip of a hood.
Unwemmed = unblemished
Vitalle = provisions
Wastle breed = expensive bread.

Webbe = weaver
Wight = person.
Wood = mad.
Wone = dwelling.
Ywis = true.

Bibliography

The Holy Bible. King James Version.

The Riverside Chaucer (Third Edition) ed. Larry D. Benson, Oxford University Press, (1987).

The Complete Works of Geoffrey Chaucer, F. N. Robinson, Second Edition, Oxford University Press. (1985)

The Piers Plowman Tradition, ed. Helen Barr, Everyman's Library, (1993).

Saul, Nigel, *Richard II*, Yale University Press, (1997)

Robertson, D. W. Jr. *A Preface to Chaucer. Studies in Medieval Perspectives*, London. OUP, (1962)

DeNeef, A. Leigh, *Robertson and the Critics,* Chaucer Review 2, (167-8), p. 207.

Fruyt and Chaff, Studies in Medieval Allegories, Bernard F. Huppe and D.W. Robertson, Jr. (1983) Princetown University Press.

Hughes, Dorothy, Illustrations of Chaucer's England, London, (1918).

The Complete Works of William Shakespeare, Ed. W. J. Craig, Oxford, (1947).

Tuchman, Barbara W., <u>A Distant Mirror. The Calamitous 14th Century</u>. Penguin Books, (1979)

<u>Froissart Chronicles</u>. Selected and Translated and Edited by Geoffrey Brereton, Penguin Books, 1968.

Woolf, Rosemary, Chaucer: See <u>A Critical Anthology</u>. Edited by J.A. Burrow, Penguin Books. Reprinted 1982.

Tyrwhitt, Thomas, *The Poetical Works of Geoffrey Chaucer*, London, (1883).

The Dictionary of National Biograhphy (DNB), Edited by Sir Leslie Stephen and Sir Sidney Lee, Smith and Elder, London. (1887).

Crow and Olson, *Chaucer Life-Records,* Oxford, (1966).

Coredon, Christopher, <u>A Dictionary of Medieval Terms and Phrases</u>, 2OO4, D.S. Brewer, Cambridge. (pp. 70-71)

Lawrence, W. W., <u>Chaucer and the Canterbury Tales</u>, Columbia University Press, New York (1964) p. 5.

Skeat, Walter W., <u>Chaucer's Minor Poems</u>, Oxford. Clarendon Press. MDCCCLXXVIII. (pp. lxxviii – lxxix)

Parr, Johnstone, *The Date and Revision of*
.

Chaucer's Knight's Tale, PMLA 60, 1945, (pp. 307-24)

Greek Lyrics, trans. Richard Lattimore, Chicago, (1975).

Greek Lyrics, trans. Richard Lattimore, Chicago, (1975).

Jones, Terry, *Chaucer's Knight*, London, (1980).

Brewer's *Dictionary of Phrase and Fable*, Cassell Publishers, (1992).

Bruce, Marie Louise, *The Usurper King: Henry of Bolingbroke 1366-99*, The Rubicon Press, (n.d.).

English Historical Documents, Richard the Second, Vol IV 1327-1485, Eyre and Spottiswood, (1969).

Bevan, Bryan, *King Richard II*, London, (1990).

The Odyssey of Homer, trans. Alexander Pope, London. (n.d.).

Lives of the Philosophers, Diogenes Laertius, (200-250 A.D.).

St George's Chapel Windsor, Sir George Bellew, London, (n.d.).

Parr, J. "*The Date and Revision of Chaucer's Knight's Tale,*" PMLA, 60, (1945).

The Politics and Economics of Aristotle, London, (1885).

Spenser, Poetical Works, eds. J. C. Smith and E. De Selincourt, Oxford UP, (1970).

Elizabethan History Plays, ed. William A. Armstrong, Oxford (1965).

English Morality Plays and Moral Interludes, eds. Edgar T. Schell and J. D. Shuchter, New York, (1969).

Lloyd, G.E.R., Aristotle: The Growth And Structure Of His Thought, Cambridge UP, (1968).

Hotson, J. Leslie, "*Col-foxVs. Chauntecleer*," PMLA, XXXIX, 762ff.).

How Reynard Caught Chanticleer, Originals and Analogues, Chaucer Society, F. J. Furnivall, Edmund Brock, and W.A. Coulston, London, (1888).

Langland's Piers the Plowman and Richard the Redeless, ed. Walter Skeat, Vol. 1, Text, Oxford, (1979).

Lewis, P. S., *Later Medieval France: The Polity*, London, (1968).

The Odes of Horace, trans. James Miche, Harmondsworth, (1978).

Piehler, Paul, *The Visionary Landscape*, Edward Arnold, (1971).

See the poem "*Truthe, Reste, and Pes*", *TEAMS Texts*, Western Michigan University.

Cicero, *On The Good Life*, Penguin Classics, (1971). Translated with an introduction by Michael Grant.

Medieval Literary Criticism, Translations and Interpretations, Edited by O.B. Hardison, Jr., Frederick Ungar Publishing Co., New York, (1984)

The Elizabethan World Picture, E.M.W. Tillyard, Penguin Books, (1975).

Loxton, H., *Pilgrimage to Canterbury*, David & Charles (Publishers) Ltd. 1978.

Coombes, H., *Literature and Criticism*, Pelican Books, 1963. (p. 8)

Krochallis, Jeanne E., *Hoccleve's Chaucer Portrait,* The Chaucer Review, Vol. 21, No. 2, (p. 240) 1986, Pennsylvania Sate Univesity Press.

Thynne, Francis, *Animadversions*, Now Newly Edited from the MS. in the Bridgewater Library by G. H. Kingsley, M.D., London, MDCCCLXV. P. 7.

Bishop, Ian, *The Narrative Art of the Canterbury Tales*, Everyman's Library, London, (1988)

Bell. Robert, *Poetical Works of Geoffrey Chaucer, Vol. 1* (pp 10-11), London, Charles Grifins and Co., Stationary Hall Court. (n.d.)

Manly, John Matthews, *Some New Light On Chaucer*, (1915), p. 67.

Cannon, Christopher, *Raptus in the Chaumpaigne Release and a Newly Discovered Document Concerning the Life of Geoffrey Chaucer*, Speculum 68 (January, 1993), pp. 74-94.

Burrow, J.A., *Medieval Writers and Their Work,* Middle English Literature and its *Background 1100-1500*. Oxford University Press, (p. 16) 1982.